Wood Finishing Fixes

Quick Answers to Over 175 Most Frequently Asked Questions

Michael Dresdner

Photography by **Sandor Nagyszalanczy**

The Taunton Press

Text © 2003 by Michael Dresdner
Photographs © 2003 by Sandor Nagyszalanczy
Illustrations © 2003 by The Taunton Press, Inc.

The Taunton Press
Inspiration for hands-on living®

The Taunton Press, Inc., 63 South Main Street, PO Box 5506, Newtown, CT 06470-5506
e-mail: tp@taunton.com
Distributed by Publishers Group West

Editor: Marilyn Zelinsky Syarto
Cover design: Howard Grossman
Interior design: Deborah Kerner / Dancing Bears Design
Photographer: Sandor Nagyszalanczy

Library of Congress Cataloging-in-Publication Data
Dresdner, Michael M.
  Wood finishing fixes : quick answers to over 175 most frequently asked
questions / Michael Dresdner.
     p. cm.
  ISBN 1-56158-591-2
  1. Wood finishing--Miscellanea. I. Title.
  TT325 .D737 2003
  684'.084--dc21
                              2003007363

Printed in the United States of America
10 9 8 7 6 5 4 3 2

The following manufacturers/names appearing in Wood *Finishing Fixes* are trademarks:
Varathane®, SealCoat®, B-I-N®, PERMA-WHITE®, DEFT®, Clear Wood Finish®, WATCO®, Waterlox®, Zinsser Bulls Eye®, Zinsser 1-2-3®, Kilz®, Wolman®, F&P®, Wolman EX-TREME®, Butcher's® Wax, Briwax®, Sherwin-Williams® Anchor-Bond, Wunderfil™, Rockler®, Bondo®, Cover-Stain®, SYNTOX®, Purdy®, 3M® Company, Nylox®, Chinex®, Taklon®, Sprig®, Penetrol®, Floetrol®, Safest Stripper™, Q-Tips®, Minwax Jacobean®, Sherwin-Williams® Gilsonite, Mohawk®, Behlen®, Buick®, Denver Broncos®, Minwax Polyshades®, Murphy's® Oil Soap, Briwax 2000®, Apollo®, Binks®, DeVilbis®, Real Milk Paint™, RPM™, Rustoleum®, Turbinaire®.

■ Working wood is inherently dangerous. Using hand or power tools improperly or ignoring safety practices can lead to permanent injury or even death. Don't try to perform operations you learn about here (or elsewhere) unless you're certain they are safe for you. If something about an operation doesn't feel right, don't do it. Look for another way. We want you to enjoy the craft, so please keep safety foremost in your mind whenever you're in the shop.

To Kaitlin, whose power, courage, and resolve while beating cancer inspired and amazed me;

Drew, a man with quiet strength, an astounding voice, and the kindest, gentlest soul I know;

and Jane, life's perfect companion.

Acknowledgments

First and foremost, I'm especially grateful to Terry Nelson, my dear and stalwart friend, who acted as my "first reader," reviewer, and prop assistant. He offered far more help than I had any right to request. Thanks, Terry. You were absolutely indispensable.

Special thanks are also due my close friend, Sandor Nagyszalanczy, for his artistry and commitment in photographing this book as well as my last two books. Thanks for yet another outstanding job.

Others who lent a hand (or two) include:

Dan Andrews	Gene Hoyas	Bruce Scheider
Bill Boxer	Peter Lyon	Dwayne Siever
John Brock	Berj Martin	Keith Tryon
Bill Cogswell	Peter McCusker	Mike Williams
Susan Cross	Chris Minick	Greg Williams
Patrick Edwards	Eric Mulford	
Ronnie Holman	J R Reding	

and several companies including:

Apollo	Purdy	Turbinaire
Behlen	Real Milk Paint	Varathane
Binks	Rockler	Watco
DeVilbiss	RPM	Wolman
Mohawk	Rustoleum	Zinsser

"If you have knowledge, let others light their candles in it."
—MARGARET FULLER, 1810–1850

Contents

Introduction

The time has come for a finishing book that answers your finishing questions as they arise, instead of forcing you to read an entire textbook on finishing. After all, when you are trying to put out a fire, you don't want a comprehensive treatise on fire control. You want a fire extinguisher.

That is precisely what this book is. It is a collection of the most commonly asked finishing questions, divided into logical chapters, with clear, concise answers on how to avoid finishing problems and how to fix finishing problems. It answers the questions you have about finishing just the way you ask them. When you have a problem, simply look up the solution. Isn't that better than having to read a whole book to find out one fact?

Wood Finishing Fixes should get you out of almost any jam during the finishing process, but as you can see by its size, it does not go into great detail. If you need a more in-depth discussion on how to accomplish some of the techniques alluded to in these pages, you'll find the answers in *The New Wood Finishing Book* or *Build Like a Pro®: Painting and Finishing*. Both books give more complete descriptions of exactly how to choose, apply, color, rub out, and repair finishes. But keep *Wood Finishing Fixes* in the workshop within easy reach, and it will save you time and aggravation when finishing your projects.

On the off chance that I still have not covered your most pressing question, don't worry. Go to my home page, "Ask Dresdner," at *www.michael-dresdner.com* and click on the "Consulting" button. E-mail your question to me, and I'll make sure you get the answer.

A note on safety

All finishing brings with it some risks. Carefully read the labels and safety warnings on all finish cans, and protect yourself with the appropriate safety equipment. If you are not sure, err on the side of safety with gloves, goggles, a respirator, and good ventilation. Ultimately, it is up to you to decide what is and is not safe. Becoming a great finisher takes lots of practice, and I want you to arrive at that point with your health intact.

—Michael Dresdner

The Right Finish

Q **How do I choose a finish? I see rows of cans at the store, and I have no idea where to start.**

A *Good question. You choose a finish by answering three basic questions: What must the finish endure, how should it look, and how do I want to apply it?*

First and foremost, a finish needs to live up to the demands put upon it. You may like the look of an ultrathin, easy-to-apply wax finish, but that won't protect a kitchen table from hard wear and frequent cleaning. List the assaults a finish will be called upon to endure (water, heat, stains, solvents, abrasion, and acids/bases), and find a finish that will hold up to them. The scorecard below will help.

The thickness of a finish is also important. Several coats of any finish will offer more protection than one thin coat. On the other hand, layering on too much finish can cause premature cracking. Four brushed coats, 6 to 8 sprayed ones, or 12 wipe-on wipe-off coats are all reasonable limits.

Choosing a look is easier. Solvent-based coatings warm up the hue of wood by adding a slight amber cast to the color. Oil-based materials enhance the depth and richness of the wood by adding even more amber color. Water-based coatings add no color and will keep white woods white because they lack the oil's ability to add an amber depth to the wood.

Most finishes can be applied in a variety of ways. Shellac, Danish oil, oil varnish, or polyurethane can be applied by hand, brush, or spray gun. Water-based coatings work well with brushes, paint pads, and spray guns. Lacquer is usually formulated for spraying, but there are versions available that can be brushed onto wood. Popular gel urethanes are designed to be wiped on because they are too thick for brushes or spray guns.

MATERIAL	WATER	HEAT	SOLVENTS	STAINS	ACIDS/ BASES	ABRASION
Wax	Poor	Poor	Poor	Poor	Poor	Poor
Linseed/ tung oil	Poor	Good	Good	Poor	Good	Poor
Danish oil	Fair	Good	Good	Poor	Good	Poor
Shellac	Good	Poor	Fair	Good	Excellent/ Poor	Good
Lacquer	Good	Poor	Fair	Good	Good	Good
Water-based	Good	Fair	Fair	Good	Good	Good
Varnish	Good	Good	Good	Good	Good	Good
Oil poly	Good	Excellent	Excellent	Good	Good	Excellent

Q. I'm not sure which finish I should use on which wood. Is there a rule of thumb I can go by?

A. You can usually apply any finish to any type of wood. Usage, not the type of wood, dictates the best finish for the job.

The finish on each of these items was based not on the type of wood but on the durability and appearance requirements of each piece.

With astonishingly few exceptions, you can apply any finish to any type of wood. It would seem logical that certain finishes work only on certain woods and not others, but in fact, just the opposite is true.

The most important issues when choosing a wood finish are durability and appearance. A table- or bar top will need a finish that offers more stain, heat, and scratch resistance than the finish for a picture frame.

Though any finish can go on any wood, admittedly one could argue that some finishes look better on some woods. But that is a matter of personal taste. Consider which finish will bring out the character of the wood that matters to you most. Oils will add depth, richness, and an amber color. So you may choose an amber oil-based coating to bring out the highlights in walnut. Water-based coatings will not bring out a wood's highlights, so you may decide to use that type of finish to keep a piece of maple as white as possible. Solvent-based coatings generally fall between the two in terms of appearance.

The two notable wood exceptions that have special finish needs are certain species of aromatic cedar, and those exotics that belong to the genus *dalbergia* (Indian rosewood, Brazilian rosewood, Honduras rosewood, cocobolo, African blackwood, kingwood, and tulipwood). These woods inhibit oxygen polymerization and can prevent oil-based varnish and polyurethane from properly curing. In some cases, aromatic cedar has been known to soften cured finishes. Avoid oil-based finishes for these particular woods, or, seal them first with dewaxed shellac or Zinsser Bulls Eye SealCoat.

Any finish will work on most any wood. This polyurethane, for instance, works equally well on these pau ferro, maple, and walnut boards.

Q **I**'m finishing a chest of drawers with Danish oil.
Should I finish the inside of the drawers the same
way, or leave them raw?

A *Leave the drawers unfinished, or use something that will
seal the wood but not impart any odor to the clothing
they will contain.*

Professional finishers almost never finish the sides or insides of drawers. Instead, they mask them when coating the fronts and leave them
unfinished. Since they are protected within the casework, there's no
need for finish. There's always the danger that the odor of a finish
will be transferred to the contents in a drawer.

However, if you prefer the smooth look and feel of sealed wood,
there are products without a lingering odor. My favorite finish is shellac, but you can also use lacquer or a water-based coating. Avoid oil,
Danish oil, and oil varnishes, as they can smell for months or longer.

When finishing a
chest, mask off the
insides of the draw-
ers and leave them
unfinished.

Q **W**ill finishing a cedar chest destroy its aroma?
Can I renew the aroma when it starts to fade?

A *Leave the chest unfinished inside, and if the aroma starts
to fade, simply sand the wood to renew the fragrance.*

Leave cedar linings
unfinished, and
renew the aroma
periodically by
sanding the surface
lightly.

Leave the cedar chest unfinished to keep the
cedar fragrance. Any finish will either fight with
the aromatic cedar aroma or entirely block it.
(You'll also want to leave it unfinished to get the
benefit of its moth-chasing abilities.) If the chest
starts to lose its cedar aroma, sand it lightly with
220-grit paper to restore its bouquet.

Aromatic cedar is typically used only to line
the inside of a hope chest, but sometimes the
whole chest is made of cedar. In that case, finish
the outside with shellac, lacquer, or water-based
coatings. Or you can first seal the wood with a
coat of dewaxed shellac or SealCoat, then use an
oil-based coating.

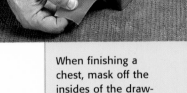

What are the advantages and disadvantages of a water-based polyurethane and lacquer versus an oil-based polyurethane and lacquer?

Neither is better or worse, and they are similar in durability, but each has its strengths and weaknesses. You need to decide which characteristics fit your needs.

It's a bit like asking if a pickup truck is better or worse than a sports car. It depends on what you intend to haul. Water-based and oil-based products are similar in durability, but each has its strengths and weaknesses. You need to decide which of the products' characteristics fit your needs.

Water-based coatings have certain strengths that make them ideal for some projects, and other characteristics that put them at a disadvantage when compared to oil- or solvent-based coatings. Water-based coatings are nonflammable, water-clear, and have fewer solvents than do oil or solvent-based coatings. Oil- and solvent-based coatings are typically flammable, amber in color, and higher in solvents. Oils and solvent lacquers bring out the depth and richness in wood, a characteristic called chatoyance. However, water-based coatings won't add any color to the wood.

Water-based and oil-based coatings are both durable. Water-based lacquer is about as durable as solvent-based lacquer, but water-based polyurethane is not quite as tough as oil-based polyurethane. Oil-based polyurethane has the edge when it comes to its ability to resist heat and chemicals. Both are equally easy to apply, though they require different techniques for brushing and spraying. Water-based polyurethane dries faster than oil-based, but solvent-based lacquer dries faster than water-based lacquer. The chart below can help you decide which product to purchase in terms of color, flammability, odor, chatoyance, and drying speed.

MATERIAL	COLOR	FLAMMABLE	SOLV. ODOR	CHATOYANCE	DRY SPEED
Water-based	Clear	No	Low	Poor	Fast
Oil-based	Amber	Most are	Medium	Excellent	Slow
Solvent-based	Light amber	Yes	Strong	Good	Very fast

Q What's a hand-rubbed varnish, and when do I use it as a finish?

A *The term is ambiguous and archaic because any modern oil varnish can be applied or rubbed by hand.*

Any modern oil varnish can be applied or rubbed by hand. Hand-rubbed varnish is an overused term that has lost any real meaning. In the old days, finishers rubbed drying oil onto wood with the palms of their bare hands, a slow and arduous task that slowly built up very thin layers of finish. Application followed the twice rule: First, apply a coat twice a day for a week, then twice a week for a month, then twice a month for a year, and finally, twice a year for life.

Over time, finishers began to switch to thicker varnishes applied by brush, which build up fast on wood. To eliminate brush marks and mimic that old, hand-rubbed look, modern finishers often rub out the last coat with abrasive pastes. Once it is dry and cured, any varnish or polyurethane can be hand rubbed to satin or gloss. Oil varnish or polyurethane can be applied by hand, as well.

One of my favorite techniques is to use a fine nylon abrasive pad to apply oil-based varnish or polyurethane. No thinner is needed. Just dip the pad into the finish, scrub it onto the wood with the pad, and wipe off any excess with paper shop towels. It gives you a thin, foolproof, natural look in minutes with no brushes or spray guns to clean. You can build up as many coats as you'd like, applying only one coat per day. Years later, if the finish starts to wear thin, add more coats the same way.

Step one: Scrub a liberal amount of varnish or polyurethane onto the wood surface with a fine nylon abrasive pad.

Step two: Immediately wipe off all excess with shop towels. Let each coat dry overnight.

Can I use exterior primer indoors on painted built-in furniture? Can I use interior primer outdoors?

Yes, you can use exterior primer—and paint—indoors, but not the other way around.

You can use exterior primer and paint indoors, but I don't advise that you use interior products outside, especially on siding. Shellac-based primers, which work like champs indoors, may form too efficient a vapor seal for siding, which can cause blistering and other problems related to trapped moisture.

Interior paint will seem to work outside initially, but it won't hold up to the rigors of outdoor exposure. The paint may fade, prematurely wear away, start to look chalky, or develop mold and mildew.

You can use exterior primer on indoor projects, but don't use interior primer outdoors.

I finished a table with Watco Danish oil, but I think it needs more protection. Can I go over it with varnish or polyurethane?

Yes, you can go over it with varnish or polyurethane, but make sure you let the Danish oil dry first.

Oils are compatible with other oils. You can go over Watco or any Danish oil with another oil varnish, including polyurethane. As with any finish, make sure one coat is dry before starting another one. Under most conditions, that means letting the finish sit overnight in a warm room.

You can also go over Danish oil with water-based polyurethane, but you should add a tie coat first. Water-based coatings won't stick to oils, but inserting a coat of Zinsser Bulls Eye SealCoat or wax-free shellac will tie the two together. Again, the oil must be dry before you brush on the shellac or SealCoat.

The author adds a few wiped-on coats of polyurethane to provide more protection for this tabletop, which was originally finished with Danish oil.

What finish is tough enough for a bar top or kitchen table? Both will get rough use, so I need something durable.

Use oil-based polyurethane for brush or hand application and conversion varnish for spraying the finish on a bar top or table.

Bar tops and kitchen tables get the worst of it. They must endure hot coffeepots, food stains like mustard and wine, acidic citrus juices, ammonia-based cleaners, alcohol spills, and plenty of scratches and dents. You need something tough enough to resist scratches, chemicals, heat, solvents, and stains.

The toughest brushable finish, and the one I would recommend in this case, is oil-based polyurethane. Water-based polyurethane runs a close second, but it does not have quite the heat or solvent resistance that an oil-based polyurethane offers. Brush on at least three or four coats of polyurethane for adequate protection. You can also wipe on polyurethane, but you will need many more coats to get the same buildup. Figure that one brushed coat is equivalent to at least four wipe-on coats. You can thin the polyurethane with about 15 percent mineral spirits for brushing, but don't thin for wipe-on application or you will need even more coats. Whether you brush or wipe, stick to one coat per day for best results.

If you are set up for spraying lacquer, another excellent option is conversion varnish or catalyzed lacquer. Both terms refer to similar two-part acid-cured finishes. They spray and dry exactly like lacquer, but will cure over time to a highly durable finish that is at least as tough as polyurethane. Conversion varnish is the preferred finish for commercial kitchen cabinets.

Polyurethane will resist wear, stains, heat, and chemicals—it's even durable enough for this toilet seat.

Make sure you accurately mix a measured amount of catalyst into a can of conversion varnish or the finish won't cure properly.

Q **Which finish is appropriate for bookshelves or living room cabinets?**

A *Most any clear or painted finish is fine for bookshelves, cabinets, and other living room furniture that is gently used.*

Bookshelves, cabinets, and other living room furniture experience gentle usage, so most any clear or painted finish will work. Other than dusting, and knickknacks, books, and tapes being moved around, there's not much wear on bookshelves and cabinets. The finish does not have to endure heat, chemicals, stains, or even water. That leaves the door wide open for you to choose a finish based on how you want the furniture to look and how you want to apply the material.

Anything from a simple, woody-looking wipe-on finish like Danish oil to several brushed-on coats of polyurethane will work. Pick the look you want—open-grained and woody, a thin film, or thick and glossy—and then choose the finish and application method that appeals to you. For thin, woody finishes, either a Danish oil mixture or a coat of shellac followed by paste wax will look great. To get a bit more buildup of film, use a couple of coats of shellac, lacquer, water-based coating, or polyurethane. Build up as much as you want, then rub to either a satin or gloss sheen.

When you want a solid color, prime the raw wood with Zinsser B-I-N, Zinsser 1-2-3, or Kilz. Follow that with as many coats as you want of colored lacquer or oil-based enamel. Avoid latex wall paint on furniture, as it will wear, show dirt, and be difficult to clean. If you prefer to work with water-based materials, opt for window and trim paint or scrubbable kitchen and bath paint.

Bookshelves get very little wear, so any coating is durable enough, even a thin coat of this brushing lacquer.

Feel free to choose water- or oil-based polyurethane, shellac, lacquer, or any finish you prefer for bookshelves.

Q: I'm making matching cabinets for the bathroom and kitchen. Since the cabinets will be subject to heat and moisture, what is the best finish to use?

Both water-based and oil-based polyurethane will work well, but be sure you seal the insides and backs of the bathroom pieces.

Mildew-proof paint, like this Perma-White brand, is designed especially for the rigors of bathrooms and kitchens. It's tough enough for a bath's wood window trim.

Kitchens are less problematic than bathrooms. You can get away with using lacquer on kitchen cabinets, but oil-based or water-based polyurethane are more durable. Commercial cabinets are usually coated in conversion varnish, which is a good option if you have access to spray equipment.

Bathrooms are more of a challenge. Bathroom cabinets need to be able to resist intense moisture for short periods of time, which could cause more wood movement than in any other part of the house. Therefore, the finish should be somewhat flexible. Hair sprays, perfume atomizers, and nail polish remover are other enemies the finish may encounter, so it needs to be resistant to chemicals and solvents as well. Both water-based and oil-based polyurethane will do fine in bathrooms. If you prefer a solid color, look for one of the special "mildew-proof" bathroom paints available.

Where you put the finish is just as important as what you apply to bathroom cabinets. Moisture that gets into the wood through the backs of the cabinets can cause the finish to peel. Before you install the cabinets, seal the backs and insides with at least one coat of polyurethane. Sealing the backs, even if they are going to be up against drywall, will help prevent moisture from entering the wood and delaminating the finish. Mirrors and picture frames that hang in the bathroom should get the same treatment. This is a good example of how an ounce of prevention is worth a pound of cure when it comes to bathroom cabinets.

Remember to seal the backs of wood objects, like this medicine cabinet, before you hang them in the bathroom.

What finish will protect a vanity top from nail polish and perfume spills?

For those who spray, conversion varnish is the best choice. If you plan to brush or wipe the finish, opt for an oil-based polyurethane.

Conversion varnish is a two-part spray coating that cures to an impervious film. Store-bought vanities typically are finished with a conversion varnish. For hobby finishers, oil-based polyurethane is just as good. It will resist the alcohol in perfume and the acetone in nail polish remover, both of which would attack shellac or lacquer. For the best durability, give the top at least three brushed-on coats, or a dozen wiped-on coats.

Oil-based polyurethane, or conversion varnish, will allow this vanity top to endure perfume and nail polish spills.

Neither glue spills nor clamped parts will stick to my assembly table. It's coated with polyurethane for durability, then waxed to create a nonstick surface.

What's the best finish for a new maple top on a workbench in my shop?

Leave workbenches unfinished. Finish assembly tables by wiping on polyurethane followed by wax.

Workbenches are best left unfinished, especially if you are using the bench to cut. A film finish could be counterproductive, because it may make the top too slippery and will prevent you from holding the wood still. Besides, you'll want to resand or plane the top flat at some point, and a finish will only get in the way.

I have an assembly table in my shop with two coats of oil-based polyurethane rubbed into the top that was then treated with a coat of paste wax. When I do glue-ups on it, the wax prevents the parts from sticking to the table and makes it easy to clean off errant glue. I rewax it from time to time to keep the top in good shape.

Q Which finish is best for a new wood floor that will likely have heavy foot traffic?

Oil-based or water-based polyurethane will do on a high-traffic floor, but waterborne Danish Finish is better.

Floors really get the worst of it. For one thing, people walk on them, something they rarely do on other finished wood. Things get spilled, dragged, and dropped, and to top it off, the wood itself moves as moisture rises up through the floor. High-traffic floors need a finish that is tough enough to resist scuffing, abrasion, and stains from spills, and flexible enough to tolerate the wood movement. That's a lot to ask.

Both water-based and oil-based polyurethane will handle the load, but the traffic will take its toll on them. Choose a satin or semigloss finish. Avoid a gloss finish because it will quickly show scuff marks. Two coats will be adequate, but you're better off with a third coat. Even then, expect to recoat the floor every three to five years.

Danish Finish, though more expensive, is better for high-traffic floors than polyurethane. This water-based coating is a one-package self-curing mixture. That means you don't have to mix anything, but after you spread it on the floor, it goes through a chemical change and cures to a highly durable film. It is just as easy to apply as any water-based coating, and it dries just as fast, but Danish Finish will last twice as long as polyurethane before it needs to be renewed. You can find it at outlets that supply flooring contractors, along with the sanders you'll need to rent for the job.

I have some words of caution about finishing floors. Let the floor cure for several days before you walk on it, and if you use any water-based coating, don't wet-mop it for the first month.

Wait a month after applying the finish before using a wet mop or cleaners on the floor.

Either oil-based polyurethanes, such as this Varathane floor finish, or Danish Finish, a special water-based reactive floor coating, will hold up on high-traffic floors.

Q I'd like to preserve the wood color on a new cedar deck and cedar fence. What finish should I use?

A Stick with penetrating deck sealer for the deck, but go with an acrylic wood siding sealer for the fence.

Scrub the deck with TSP and bleach to remove dirt and mildew. Let it dry thoroughly before coating.

Decks are exposed to weather and trod upon all year. You will want a flexible finish that can tolerate lots of wood movement, yet is tough enough to resist scuffing. However, there is no such perfect finish.

But there is a compromise. A clear deck coating is your best choice. The coating penetrates into the wood rather than forming a film on top. Since there is no topical coating of film to crack, peel, chip, or scuff, the wood continues to look good through foot traffic and seasonal wood movement.

Deck coatings come both clear and semi-transparent (lightly pigmented) in common wood colors. Choose a coating that contains UV blockers or absorbers to stave off sun damage. In addition, look for a coating with mildewcide and fungicide to prevent mold growth. My favorite is an oil-based coating from Wolman called F&P, but there are many excellent brands in both water-based and oil-based formats.

Keep the deck looking good by cleaning it and reapplying deck coating every year. After several years of diligence, it's okay to skip a year, but bite the bullet and commit to routine care in the beginning of the deck's life.

As for the fence, which only gets walked on by squirrels and the family cat, I'd suggest a 100 percent acrylic water-based wood siding sealer, such as Wolman Extreme. It can be easily applied to wet wood, dry wood, and even pressure-treated posts. Don't be surprised if you don't need to touch it up again for five years.

If you live in a region where mildew is a problem, add extra mildewcide to your favorite deck coating.

How should I finish teak Adirondack chairs and a mahogany front door?

Use spar varnish for clear coatings, and exterior trim paint if you decide you'd rather the chair and doors match the color of the house.

Patio furniture, exterior doors, planters, and outdoor ornamental items like birdhouses are best finished with good old-fashioned spar varnish. Authentic spar varnish, which is a combination of tung oil and phenolic resin, has two characteristics that make it ideal for exterior projects. First, the ingredients have a natural resistance to ultraviolet light. That does not mean the clear finish will prevent the wood below it from getting lighter or darker from sun exposure. It merely means that the coating itself will not degrade due to sunlight. Second, it tends to fail from the top down. Many finishes degrade at the wood interface, causing them to peel and necessitating total refinishing. Spar varnish gets dull on top, at which point you can simply sand the surface and add another coat, which adheres nicely to the old varnish.

Wiping or brushing on several coats of spar varnish will keep wood looking good and easy to clean. The coating will last several years, but all outdoor coatings need some routine maintenance. Clean them and remove surface mildew each spring. Add another coat every few years or whenever the surface shows signs of wear.

If you decide to paint the wood a solid color, prime the wood with an exterior water-based primer, then top it off with 100 percent acrylic exterior trim paint. This is a great opportunity to have the front door, or even the patio furniture, match the house's trim color.

My mahogany Adirondack chairs are finished with several coats of spar varnish.

Spar varnish is also a perfect finish for the front door. Add another coat when you notice the finish starting to wear.

What's the best finish for interior doors and millwork?

Use trim paint for solid color, and shellac, lacquer, oil, varnish, and polyurethane for clear coatings on interior doors and millwork.

If you want to paint interior doors and millwork a solid color, use trim paint. For clear finishes, you have your choice of shellac, lacquer, oil, varnish, and polyurethane.

Painting doors and millwork in solid colors is simple. Prime the wood with an interior alcohol-based or water-based primer, then coat it with either oil-based or water-based trim paint. Trim paints are more durable and easier to clean than regular flat wall paint.

If you prefer a clear finish on doors and millwork, you'll have a wide range of choices. Interior millwork is not subject to many abrasions or spills, stains, or chemicals, so as a result, most any finish will do. For a semiunfinished look, use a few coats of tung, boiled linseed, or Danish oil to simply seal the wood. This treatment will help the wood keep its color while leaving the surface feeling nearly unfinished. If you prefer a more traditional look, use two coats of either shellac, lacquer, or oil varnish to add depth and sparkle to the wood. Oil-based polyurethane is just as appropriate, and a bit more durable. If you have very light-colored wood and want to keep it that way, use water-based polyurethane. Unlike the solvent-based alternatives, it goes on clear and will not yellow with age.

Doors generally suffer from more handling. While any of the above-mentioned finishes are appropriate for doors, in most cases, I would lean toward the tougher polyurethanes. Two or three coats will give you a finish that will endure the scuffs, scrapes, and the extra cleanings that a well-used door will experience. Pay special attention to the area around the handle and non-hinged edge, because these areas are handled and scratched more frequently.

You'll avoid drips if you take the door off the hinges and set it horizontally on sawhorses.

Most any finish will work for interior millwork. Mask the adjacent walls first to keep them clean.

Q What's the safest finish for a baby's crib?

*Shellac is considered the safest finish for a baby's crib,
but most other common finishes are safe enough.*

Most common finishes are safe, but shellac is undoubtedly the safest finish for a piece of baby furniture. Once dry, shellac is completely edible. In fact, the vast majority of shellac sold in this country is used to coat food, fruit, candy, vitamins, and drugs. If a baby chewed on the finish—and many do—no harm would be done, at least to the baby.

As for other coatings, once dried, just about every common finish is inert and indigestible. Eating bits of finish would be equivalent to swallowing bits of plastic that go right through your system. So varnish, polyurethane, lacquer, and even paint are all fair game for cribs.

Of course, boiled linseed oil, Danish oil, and some oil varnishes contain heavy-metal salts added to speed up the drying time of the mixture. One could argue that these make the cured finish toxic. However, driers are added in such small percentages that a child would have to consume a tremendous amount of finish for that to be an issue.

Today, painted cribs are also safe. Decades ago, paint was often formulated with lead. Since the lead compounds in paint taste slightly sweet, there were cases of children munching on paint chips, a habit that could lead to lead poisoning. Because of the safety issue, manufacturers stopped putting lead in paint back in 1978.

If you are worried, use shellac and sleep easy. Otherwise, use whatever you like. If it helps, I can tell you that I have never heard of a single case of a child being poisoned by chewing on any modern clear coating.

SealCoat is actually a shellac, an edible, food-safe (and baby-safe) finish.

Q I make cutting boards and wooden spoons. What finish is best for items that come in contact with food?

A Cutting boards can remain unfinished, but if you prefer a finish, various oils and waxes will enhance the appearance of the piece for a little while.

A cutting board that is frequently used and washed does not need a finish. In fact, there is no finish that would hold up on a cutting board. I use lots of wooden utensils and cutting boards, and they all hold up well without any finishes on them at all.

The problem is that raw wood doesn't look as pretty as wood that is enhanced with oil. That leads folks to want to dress up cutting boards and spoons before they give them away as gifts. Though it's fine to do that, know that whatever finish you put on the item will come off with use.

Edible mineral oil is a common treatment for food items, but it is a nondrying oil and will stay wet as long as it is on (or rather "in") the wood. Each time you wash the board with soap and water, you will be removing a good bit of the mineral oil. To keep it looking good, you must constantly reoil it. A thin coat of a drying oil on the wood, like linseed, walnut, or tung oil, will last longer, but it too will eventually wear away. The same is true for wax, which will eventually rub off.

Chopping blocks like the ones that butchers use are all end grain, and they are a different story. The traditional treatment for chopping blocks is to pour melted paraffin wax into the end grain, and then after the wax hardens, to scrape off whatever the pores did not absorb.

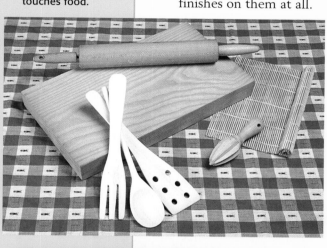

These items from my kitchen are all left unfinished, the best choice for wood that touches food.

Edible mineral oil will enhance the color in wood, but it will soon wash off with use.

Q **W**hich finishes will go over other finishes? For instance, can I put lacquer over shellac or polyurethane over Danish oil?

A *Most clear finishes will go over most other clear finishes.*

Clear finishes generally work well together, with few exceptions. For example, don't put new lacquer over old varnish that is flexible or thick, or the entire finish is likely to crack or wrinkle. Avoid putting water-based coatings or oil-based polyurethane over shellac; if the shellac contains wax the finish could delaminate. You can get around this problem, and most other compatibility issues, by using a coat of SealCoat first. The chart below will help you determine which finishes are safe to coat over other finishes.

OVER / UNDER	OILS (GO OVER)	VARNISH	LACQUER	SHELLAC (W/WAX)	SEALCOAT (NO WAX)	WATER-BASED
Oils	Yes	Yes	Yes	Yes	Yes	No
Varnish	Yes	Yes	No	Yes	Yes	No
Lacquer	Yes	Yes	Yes	Yes	Yes	Yes
Shellac	No	No	Yes	Yes	Yes	No
SealCoat	Yes	Yes	Yes	Yes	Yes	Yes
Water-based	Yes	Yes	Yes	Yes	Yes	Yes

Can I add a coat of clear polyurethane on top of latex paint to make it more durable?

You can add a coat of clear polyurethane on top of latex paint for durability, but it is probably not the best solution to the problem.

Both oil-based and water-based polyurethane will adhere to latex paint. Water-based polyurethane is clear, so it won't change the color of the paint, but oil-based polyurethane is amber, and will alter the hue, especially when used with light-color paints. For that reason, it makes more sense to use water-based polyurethane on top of latex paint unless you are intentionally trying to make the paint look more amber in hue.

Instead of adding a coat of polyurethane over latex paint for more durability, choose specially formulated washable, scrubbable "kitchen and bath" paint.

Unless the surface is newly painted, you'll have to make sure it is clean and free of wax or grease by cleaning it with TSP (trisodiumphosphate) or TSP substitute. Follow the directions on the container, and be sure to rinse off TSP residue after cleaning. Let the wood dry thoroughly before you coat it with the clear finish.

Polyurethane, either oil-based or water-based, is more resistant to abrasion, scrubbing, and even stains than some latex paints. There are some excellent washable and scrubbable acrylic water-based paints on the market. Sold as "scrubbable kitchen paint" or sometimes "children's-room paint," they are in many ways as durable as polyurethane and may be easier to clean and more resistant to staining. Simply re-painting with one of these high-quality paints seems like a much better solution.

While we are on the subject, I'll also mention that you can put shellac over latex paint, but it won't be much more durable. But if you like the look, shellac will make the surface shiny, and it will be a little easier to clean. Don't try covering latex paint with lacquer or the paint will wrinkle.

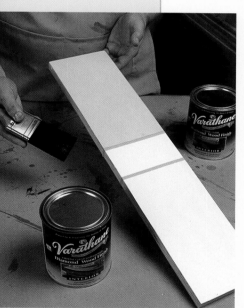

Oil-based polyurethane (top half of board) will add an amber tint to white or pastel paint. Water-based polyurethane won't change the color of the paint.

Q I'd like to paint my kitchen cabinets and chairs. Should I first strip the old finish? Then, what paint would you suggest?

A You don't have to strip an old finish if it's sound, but always use a good primer as a base, then use scrubbable paint as a new finish.

As long as the old finish on your kitchen cabinets and chairs is sound and not peeling or cracked, you can paint over it without stripping. But you should use a good primer first. After priming, use trim and kitchen paint because they are more durable and easier to clean than flat wall paints.

If you have old lacquer, varnish, polyurethane, or even the high-tech conversion varnish that's typically used for kitchen cabinets, it is not necessary to strip it off unless the old coating is cracked or peeling. The new coating may adhere to the old, but if the old one is flaking off from the wood, it will take your new coat of paint along with it.

If the old coating is in good shape, you can coat the old clear finish with oil-based enamel or with water-based paint. Although latex wall paint will stick just fine, it will not hold up to the rigors of kitchen traffic. Instead, choose an acrylic window, door, and trim paint, or one of the special scrubbable paints designed for kitchens, bathrooms, and children's rooms. Though these paints are more expensive than standard wall paint, the cost is well worth it for this application.

Start the job by cleaning the surfaces thoroughly with TSP (trisodiumphosphate) or TSP substitute. Rinse the surfaces well, let them dry, and lightly sand with 220-grit paper to smooth them while scoring any glossy areas. Wipe off the sanding dust and apply a coat of high-quality primer, such as Zinsser Bulls Eye BIN. The BIN will dry in just a few hours, after which you can paint. The chairs get the same treatment.

A sound finish can be cleaned and repainted without stripping, but first, start with a primer coat of BIN.

Treat kitchen chairs the way you would finish cabinets. Clean them first, then apply BIN before painting to ensure good adhesion.

Q When do I use wax as a finish? What types of wax should I consider for which project?

A *Any brand of wax will work for pieces that get little or no wear.*

Wax is both the easiest finish to apply and arguably the weakest. It offers almost no protection from abrasion, water, stains, or much of anything else. Turners like wax because it is easy to apply on the lathe, and there's no waiting time for drying. It's fine for art turnings, picture frames, ornamental boxes, and the like that will get very little wear and just need to sit there and look pretty. One note about wax is that it does not substantially change the look of wood the way oil and solvent-based finishes do.

Most paste waxes are similar, so I choose the best wax for the job based on secondary characteristics. Some waxes are a bit softer in the can, some harder, some dry faster, some slower, and some smell better. Pick the one you like to work with, because after they dry, you'll have a hard time telling them apart. I'm partial to Butcher's Wax and Briwax, but I often use whatever is handy.

To keep wax low-luster, put it on and wipe it off immediately. To add more sheen, let it dry and buff it off. Here's a great recipe for a natural-looking traditional wax finish. Seal the raw wood by flooding on a coat of shellac, then immediately wiping off whatever does not soak into the wood. Let the shellac dry a few hours, then lightly sand with 320 paper to remove the rough whiskers. Apply a coat of paste wax with 0000 steel wool, and wipe it off with paper shop towels. Now that's my idea of an authentic wax finish.

Linseed oil (right side of board) adds an amber tint to this almost white maple board. Wax (left side) lets it retain its natural color.

Apply paste wax by scrubbing it onto the wood with fine 0000 steel wool, then wiping it off with a shop towel.

Q Is Deft a finish?

Deft is a brand, not a finish, but the manufacturer's most popular offering is actually a brushing lacquer.

When most people talk about Deft, they are referring to Deft Clear Wood Finish, which is a brushing lacquer. Furniture lacquer is normally formulated for spraying, but Deft makes one of the few widely distributed brushing lacquers. It offers all the advantages of spray lacquer—quick dry times, clarity, durability, repairability, and only a hint of amber—to those who prefer to brush on their finishes. If you are experienced with brushing shellac or using fast-drying varnishes, you will be able to get a beautiful finish with Deft.

Deft now offers oil-based products including Danish oil, stains, and both interior and exterior polyurethane. But to most woodworkers, the name Deft is still synonymous with brushing lacquer.

Deft is a brand name, but the company's most famous product is a brushing lacquer called Clear Wood Finish. It's a perfect choice for this guitar.

Q What is Danish oil and is it different from Watco or Waterlox?

Danish oil is very thin varnish modified for wipe-on application. Watco and Waterlox are both brands of Danish oil.

Watco is probably the most well known brand of Danish oil, a type of thin, wipe-on finish that offers good looks but little durability.

Woodworkers who prefer to wipe on finishes use Danish oil, typically Watco and Waterlox brands. Most Danish oil formulations consist of a small amount of varnish resin for durability, some oil for easy wiping, and lots of mineral spirits to make the mixture thin.

Because Danish oil goes on in such thin coats, it offers very little protection from water, stains, and abrasion. However, if you were to build up enough coats of the Danish oil, the result would be every bit as durable as any other brushed varnish.

Q What is boiled linseed oil?

A Boiled linseed oil is merely flaxseed oil modified to make it dry faster.

Linseed oil, extracted from flaxseeds, is a drying oil, which means a thin coat will cure by itself when exposed to air. However, in its raw state it dries so slowly that one coat on wood would take about a week to dry. That makes it impractical as a wood finish. To speed it up, manufacturers add heavy-metal salts that act as catalysts to make the oil dry faster. Oil with driers added is called boiled linseed oil, in spite of the fact that it is not boiled or even heated. Where raw linseed oil takes a week, a coat of boiled linseed oil will dry overnight in a warm, dry room.

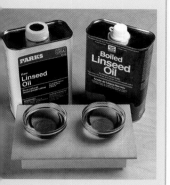

Boiled linseed oil (right) contains driers that make it cure faster than raw linseed, or flaxseed, oil (left). In all other respects, these two are identical.

Q What's the difference between linseed and tung oil, and when do I use them?

A There's little difference between linseed oil and tung oil. Linseed oil ambers slightly more than tung oil.

From a woodworker's viewpoint, there's very little difference between linseed and tung oil. Linseed oil ambers a bit more, but other than that, it's a coin toss.

Linseed and tung oils are both natural-drying oils. Both dry by taking oxygen from the air to convert from a liquid to a solid, but in their natural state, neither is very good for finishing. Raw linseed oil dries too slowly, so boiled oil is the finisher's choice. Tung oil dries faster on its own, but it is prone to wrinkling, so it is generally heat treated and sold as heat-bodied tung oil.

Both make thin, soft, amber-colored finishes that wipe on easily but offer little protection. Linseed oil tends to amber more over time than does tung oil, but other than that, they're pretty similar. Since both can be easily modified or combined with resins, they are both used in the manufacture of oil-based varnish and polyurethane.

Other than the slight color variance apparent on this board, there is little difference between tung oil and linseed oil.

Q **I see Japan drier in art supply stores, craft stores, and sometimes in woodworking specialty stores. What is it and when do I use it?**

A *Japan drier is an additive that quickly cures oil, oil varnish, and oil colors.*

Japan drier is an additive designed to speed up the cure time of oil, oil varnish, and oil colors, but adding too much of it can be counterproductive.

Heavy-metal salts are added to slow-drying oils and varnishes to speed up the cure time. They work by shuttling oxygen from the surface into the film to accelerate polymerization, the chemical reaction that forms large molecules from smaller ones. Many artists use either cobalt drier or Japan drier to speed up the drying time of oil colors.

Impatient finishers are tempted to add Japan driers to boiled linseed oil and oil varnish. That's fine, but two warnings are in order. First, adding too much drier will actually make the finish dry slowly, not faster, and may create a weaker film. Most varnishes and all boiled linseed oil already have drier added, and since you don't know how much the manufacturer put in, it is risky to dump in extra drier on your own.

The other warning has to do with how driers work and when they don't work. Very high humidity can disable the drier in a mixture, making varnish dry very slowly and causing boiled linseed oil to act like raw linseed oil. In that case, adding more drier won't do anything, but when the humidity drops, you may very well have a mixture with too much drier in it. The bottom line is that you should be very cautious about adding driers unless you are sure of what's already added to the mixture. Always test your mixture on a sample first to be sure it will behave the right way.

Japan drier can speed up the cure time of oils and oil varnish, but it must be used cautiously.

Adding too much Japan drier can actually hinder cure time, and high humidity may disable it completely. Read the container label for usage guidelines.

What are Japan colors? Are they different from artist's oil colors, and when do I use them?

Manufacturers create faster-drying Japan colors by adding driers to oil colors.

Artist's colors with driers already mixed in are called Japan colors. Use these faster-drying pastes to color oil-based filler, putty, or coatings so that adding color does not extend the drying time of your mix.

Why the name "Japan"? By the late 1800s, Japanese lacquer work was becoming popular in the United States. Because the materials used in Japan are not appropriate here, finishers developed an approximation of the enameled look to create "Japanned" furniture. The coating was a varnish consisting of pigments ground into oil with driers added. Though Japan was originally a varnish, today's Japan colors contain mostly pigment with just enough oil to act as a binder.

The only difference between Japan colors (left) and artist's oil colors (right) is in how fast they dry. Japans dry faster.

Which coatings stay clear and which finishes turn yellow over time?

Water-based coatings start out clear and stay that way over time. Lacquer and shellac amber a bit, but oils and oil varnish yellow the most.

The clearest are the water-based acrylic lacquers followed closely by water-based polyurethane, which is actually just slightly bluish-gray. Shellac and lacquer are slightly amber, then yellow a bit over time. Oil varnishes, polyurethanes, and tung oil start out amber, then deepen a bit. But the champ is linseed oil, which starts out very amber and turns a deeper hue as years go by.

Water-based coatings (left) start clear and stay that way. Oils (right) start out amber and get darker over time.

Q What is milk paint?

Milk paint is made from fresh or soured milk that has reacted with slaked lime. You can either buy it in powdered form or make it yourself.

Milk paint comes as a ready-to-mix powder in a wide range of colors.

Before home improvement stores made finishes an off-the-shelf product, people mixed their own coatings from what was at hand. One of the more durable of these was milk paint, made by reacting either fresh or curdled milk protein with slaked lime. To get a thicker, more opaque, or colored mixture, you added chalk and other pigments. If you are so inclined, you can still do that yourself.

Milk paint is often used on country period furniture to achieve a rustic farmhouse look. Colors are usually deep and dun rather than bright and vivid, since they were made from natural pigments like iron oxide, charcoal, and clay. Because the paint is chalky, finishers often seal it with clear coats of oil, shellac, or polyurethane after it is fully cured.

The paint itself is tenacious, and once applied, resists most paint removers. You can get it off with special milk paint removers or lye. It will stick to clean, sanded wood or drywall, but won't stick to oil finishes or most solvent finishes. However, you can get it to stick by first applying a binder or a tie coat of Sherwin Williams Anchor-Bond.

Two companies in the United States currently market authentic milk paint. Both offer it as a powder ready to mix with water. Because the mixed paint has a very short shelf life (it keeps typically under two weeks if it's refrigerated, and less if the mixture is kept warm), it is wise to mix only the amount that you will use. Buy milk paint from: Old Fashioned Milk Paint Co. (www.milkpaint.com or 978-448-6336) and Real Milk Paint (www.realmilkpaint.com or 800-339-9748).

Milk paint colors are deep but not shiny and are often used to create a rustic look.

Q I've seen references to "home brew" containing boiled linseed oil, turps, and poly. What is it, how do I make it, and when do I use it?

It's common to mix boiled linseed oil (BLO), turpentine (turps), and polyurethane varnish (poly) to create a home brew. But don't be too quick to jump on that bandwagon.

You can make wiping varnish by adding a cup of boiled linseed oil to a quart of varnish.

Scrubbing on straight oil-based polyurethane with a nylon abrasive pad is easier and more effective than using a home brew.

There's nothing wrong with making up your own personal mixtures. The most common ones contain about one-third of each of the above ingredients. This nets you something vaguely similar to the many Danish oil finishes on the market. However, I'd only mix my own if what I needed was not available as a commercial product, or if I could make it less expensively—or of higher quality—at home.

Let's look at what these home mixtures can accomplish. Adding boiled linseed oil to polyurethane creates a less durable finish that is slower drying but easier to spread. If that's what you want, make wiping varnish by adding a cup of boiled linseed oil to a quart of polyurethane. Pouring in turpentine merely makes the finish thinner so that more coats are needed. (Contrary to popular belief, adding turpentine or any other solvent does not make it penetrate the wood better.)

Instead of going the home-brew route, try this next time. Choose any oil-based polyurethane and stir it, but don't thin it. Dip a fine nylon abrasive pad into the finish and scrub it onto the wood. The pad will work better than a rag for moving the liquid around and getting it into the pores. Now wipe off the surface evenly, leaving only a thin, uniform coat. You will have applied the greatest amount of protective polyurethane in one wiped coat without weakening it. This technique also works with gel polyurethanes, which are really just thicker versions of polyurethane varnish.

I've always heard that oil-based paint is more durable than latex, but home improvement stores offer mostly latex products. Which is better?

Oil paint would win hands down over latex paint for durability, but many new trim paints are highly durable acrylics.

Years ago painters swore by oil-based paints, and for good reason. Oil-based paints were more durable and easier to clean than latex paint. However, you now have other choices. The best water-based trim paints, both interior and exterior, are now made with acrylic or polyurethane resins. Ask for these instead of straight latex paint. They're as durable as oils but dry faster and are less likely to blister or peel over time. In addition, you can apply them with paint pads or rollers as well as with brushes. See, you can have the best of both worlds.

Water-based acrylic trim paints offer the durability of oil paint with the convenience of latex.

Are there clear finishes that will prevent colored woods, like purpleheart, padauk, and cherry, from fading or darkening?

Some exterior coatings contain UV blockers and absorbers, but they won't entirely prevent the sun from doing its damage.

Yes, some exterior coatings contain UV blockers and absorbers that will somewhat alleviate fading or color changes. The UV (ultraviolet) portion of the sun's rays is responsible for most of the color changes that occur in finished wood. Some woods fade while others get darker. The UV rays go right through clear finishes. Invisible UV blockers and absorbers that minimize this effect are sometimes added to exterior coatings, but rarely to interior finishes. Exterior finishes that contain these additives will usually say so on the can's label. These finishes can work just as well indoors. The additives will help, but they only prolong the inevitable. Given enough time and exposure, the wood will still fade. In the end, the sun always wins.

This walnut base faded from exposure to the sun, except for the round spot, which was covered.

Q Please explain what shellac is and when it's used. I heard it's not waterproof and it's made from crushed bugs. What's the truth?

A Fresh, dewaxed shellac is waterproof, acid and stain resistant, hard, and clear. It's made by bugs, not from bugs.

Shellacs, clockwise from upper right: buttonlac, seedlac, blond, bleached, wax. Liquids in jars, left to right: regular, dewaxed, garnet. Center: Sticklac.

There's a lot of confusion about shellac, so let's start from the beginning. A small bug called laccifer lacca swarms on certain trees in India and Thailand and creates a protective shellac shell during its larva stage. Once the adult males fly off, the shell is scraped from the encrusted tree branches and crumbled. Called seedlac, it contains a natural reddish dye and about 5 percent wax along with shellac resin. The seedlac can be dissolved as is in alcohol, or the dye and wax can be removed to make blond dewaxed shellac. Shellac comes both with and without the wax in it, and in a variety of colors, though the most common are orange and blond.

Shellac gets its bad press because of its short shelf life and its problematic wax content. The longer it sits in liquid form, the more shellac deteriorates. In addition, old shellac takes longer to dry and makes a softer film that is more susceptible to water spots. The wax content found in some shellacs (shellacs are slightly waxy in their natural state) reduces their clarity and also contributes to their tendency to create water spots. On the bright side, shellac with wax adds volume to the finish.

Fresh, dewaxed shellac makes a beautiful, clear, fast-drying finish that is easy to apply and repair. It's also waterproof, hard, stain resistant, and acid-proof. It's a universal sealer because it sticks to anything (even glass), is compatible underneath any finish, and it seals in wood resin, wax, grease, dirt, and even silicone oil. The only drawbacks are poor resistance to heat, alkalines, and alcohol. Until recently, all liquid shellac contained wax, but Zinsser now offers SealCoat, a dewaxed shellac modified to give it a long shelf life. For shellac lovers like me, it's a real blessing.

SealCoat, which is dewaxed shellac, is perfect for sealing the knots in this pine board.

Preparing to Finish

Q What does prefinishing mean and when should I do it?

Prefinishing means finishing part or all of the wood before the piece is assembled, and you should do it whenever it is possible.

Prefinishing the panel before setting the frame will prevent bare wood from emerging later, and makes the finishing job easier.

If possible, it's a good idea to finish the parts before you assemble the furniture. Prefinishing allows you to work on flat, easy-to-handle parts. Sanding, brushing, wiping, spraying, and rubbing out the finish are all far simpler on small, flat surfaces than on complicated assembled pieces. When you prefinish, you won't be faced with hard-to-reach inside corners that fill up with overspray or bedevil you with puddles and runs when you brush on finishes. Best of all, when you glue up after finishing, glue squeeze-out comes right off, and you won't have ugly glue spots beneath the stain.

You can even prefinish part of your project. When you are making floating raised-panel doors, for example, finish the panels before you glue up the frame around them. Since the panels aren't glued in, you won't need to mark or mask them before finishing. The same is true for adjustable shelves in bookcases. For tables, finish the top and base separately, then attach them with screws or other mechanical fasteners.

Even joinery can be prefinished, though it may at first seem impractical. Dovetail joints, for example, are generally planed or sanded after glue-up to level the protruding pins or tails. However, I know of one expert woodworker who routinely finishes only the side of the dovetailed board that will become the inside corners of a case or box. After assembly, he must finish the outside, but the inside corners are as clean as a whistle.

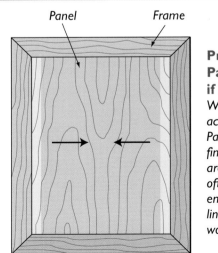

Panel   Frame

Prefinish Panels if Possible
Wood shrinks across the grain. Panels that are finished after they are in the frame often shrink enough to show a line of unfinished wood at the edges.

Q Are there any special tricks I need to know about the prefinishing process and procedure?

A Dry-fit and assemble the piece, mark the glue joints, then take it apart. Mask the glue joints with painter's tape, finish, and reassemble.

Step one: Assemble the piece and outline the joints lightly in pencil. Mask areas that will become glue surfaces.

Prefinishing steps are simple. First, sand all the parts and dry-fit them. Lightly mark the edges of the joints in pencil, then take the piece apart. In some cases, such as with shouldered tenons, there is no need to mark the wood because it is obvious that the glue will only go on the tenon cheeks.

Mask the areas that will be glue surfaces so that no finish gets on them. Use blue painter's tape and leave it on during finishing. The tape is designed to come off easily and leave no adhesive residue even after sitting on the surface for a long time. Regular masking tape will leave adhesive residue and will tear when coming off if it's left on the surface for more than a day or two.

Mask just inside the pencil line, then remove the pencil marks with alcohol or an eraser. If the masking tape is set a scant $\frac{1}{16}$ in. inside the edge of the joint, the finish will appear to go under the adjacent board and will not show an unfinished wood line. That small amount of lost glue surface will not affect the joinery, but it will give you a clean-looking finished joint.

Finally, apply the stain and finish, and if possible, rub the finish out before you do the final glue-up. Clamp gently and use clamp pads so that you do not mar the pieces during glue-up. You can always do a final wax rub afterward to even out subtle press marks.

Step two: Mask inside the line, and erase the pencil lines before finishing.

Q Does the "tack" in tack cloths interfere in any way with the finish?

Sometimes, but not usually. One safe way to avoid the issue is to use a damp cloth instead.

Most tack cloths—commonly called tack rags—don't cause problems with finishes. The sticky substance on the cloth picks up sanding dust and dirt without leaving any nasty residue. Some finishes, though, are more sensitive to even minimal contamination. Contamination problems, such as fisheye or streaking, usually occur with water-based finishes. It's rare to see problems with solvent or oil-based coatings.

If you are worried about using a tack cloth on a finish, or if you have already experienced problems with the finish you are using, there's an inexpensive and simple solution. Instead of a tack rag, use a damp cloth to pick up dust on the finish. Soak a clean cotton cloth and wring it out so that you leave it damp, but not wet. Damp means about as wet as a healthy dog's nose.

There is one more subtle but important advantage to using a damp cloth. When you work with a tack rag, it picks up dust but it also creates a static charge on the wiped surface. That charge attracts dust from the air like a magnet. The result is that new dust settles onto the surface almost as fast as you wipe it off. A damp cloth won't do that because static charges cannot exist in areas of high humidity. As a result, a surface wiped with a damp cloth stays dust-free longer than one wiped with a tack rag.

A damp cloth makes a great tack cloth. If the cloth leaves water on the surface, it is too wet.

Q **When I'm sanding bare wood, I never know whether I am sanding too much or too little. Is there a schedule I can follow?**

A *For most woods, I start sanding diagonally across the grain with 80-grit sandpaper, then I move up to 120-grit, then to 180. This schedule is followed by an additional hand sanding with the grain, using 180-grit garnet paper.*

Each step of your sanding sequence has a specific objective that will dictate the type and size of grit you'll use, when to move on to the next grit, and finally, when to stop sanding.

The objective of the first sanding is to remove machine and tool marks and flatten irregularities. I sand diagonally, using 80-grit aluminum oxide paper, which is aggressive enough to quickly achieve this goal. The purpose of the next sanding is to remove the 80-grit scratches, and I do that with 120-grit aluminum oxide paper. Follow that step with 180-grit aluminum oxide paper to remove the 120-grit scratches. For the final sanding, I sand by hand *with* the grain using 180-grit garnet paper (instead of aluminum oxide). This softens any visible scratches by blending them into the grain. This sequence will work for all but the hardest woods, such as ebony, boxwood, or rock maple. For these woods, I add another sanding step, using 220-grit garnet paper with the grain.

When any wood starts out very smooth with no tool marks, you can sometimes omit the 80-grit paper and start at 120-grit paper. These numbers are relative but not absolute. It's fine to use 100-grit, then 150-grit to 180-grit instead of the 80-, 120-, and 180- schedule. The important things to remember are that you shouldn't make too big a jump between grits and that you sand all parts of the piece with the same grit at the same time.

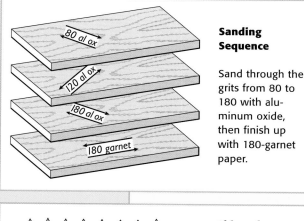

**Sanding
Sequence**

Sand through the grits from 80 to 180 with aluminum oxide, then finish up with 180-garnet paper.

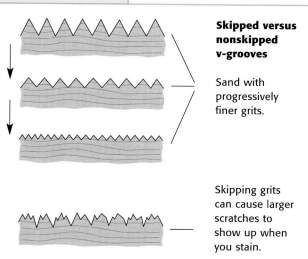

**Skipped versus
nonskipped
v-grooves**

Sand with progressively finer grits.

Skipping grits can cause larger scratches to show up when you stain.

Q I've always heard that you should sand wood with the grain, but my friend said he was told just the opposite. What's the right answer?

A *The last sanding step should always be with the grain, but all other steps should go diagonally across the grain.*

The most efficient way to level and smooth a board is by sanding diagonally across the grain with a sanding block. Sanding diagonally cuts the wood fibers fast and cleanly, and prevents a washboarding effect from happening between the soft and hard grain lines, which commonly occurs with many woods.

Each time you change grits, change diagonal directions too. The goal of each sanding is to remove the previous grit's scratches. Once all the scratches opposite your current sanding direction are gone, you are finished with that grit and ready to move on to the next grit. Finally, sand with the grain on the last sanding to remove the diagonal scratches.

Sand diagonally across the grain with all grits except the last one. The last sanding goes with the grain.

Q I use an electric ROS (random orbit sander) and often get curlicue scratches that show up after staining. How can I avoid that?

A *Curlicue scratches happen when you move the sander too fast. Move the ROS about 1 in. per second.*

Except for the last sanding, which must be done by hand, an electric random orbit sander, or palm sander, can make the job easier. An electric ROS cuts fast and flat because it sands across the grain in small circles.

Curlicue scratches, called "pigtails," are a result of moving the sander too fast. Power sanders are meant to be moved only 1 in. per second, and at that speed they won't create pigtails. Try this: Move your finger slowly enough so that it takes 8 seconds to go from one side of this page to the other. That's how fast you should be moving your sander.

Pigtail scratches mean you are moving the sander too fast or leaning on it too hard.

Q What are open-coat, self-lubricated, and wet/dry sandpapers, and which ones should I use on various projects?

A Each paper offers a characteristic that makes it ideal for a particular sanding job. Use open coat for bare wood, stearated for finish, and wet-and-dry for wet sanding.

From left to right, wet/dry, white stearated, gold stearated, garnet, and special stearated paper for latex paint.

Sandpaper is identified by the cryptic terms stamped on the back of each sheet, or on the package. Here are the most common terms and what they mean:

Closed-coat/Open-coat paper—Closed-coat sandpaper has grit covering 100 percent of the surface of the paper. Open coat has grit covering only 40 percent to 70 percent, with spaces between the grit. The spaces act like the gullets in a saw blade because they clear sanding dust (called swarf) and prevent clogging on the paper. To sand bare wood, use only open-coat paper.

Self-lubricating or "stearated" paper—In addition to the abrasive grit, stearated papers are interlaced with a soft, powdery soap called zinc stearate that lubricates the paper and the surface to make sanding easier. Use stearated papers for sanding between coats of finish. The stearate also prevents finish from forming little clots that tend to stick to paper. It is fine to use this type of paper for raw wood, but it's not necessary. Stearated paper can be gray-white or gold in color and is usually more expensive than non-stearated paper.

Wet-and-dry paper—Finishers traditionally "wet sand" when working with very fine grits. Soapy water or mineral spirits used on the waterproof paper reduces friction and carries away the sanding dust, or swarf, so that the paper does not clog or drag. Wet sanding is less common because self-lubricated paper is now available in ultra-fine grits.

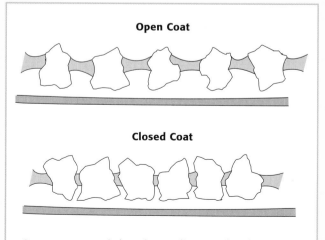

Open Coat

Closed Coat

Open-coat paper is best for sanding wood and finish.

Paper, cloth, and film are used as sandpaper backings, while garnet, aluminum oxide, and silicon carbide are grit choices. Which combination is used for which finish?

Different grit and backing combinations are best for certain tasks, and the manufacturers take that into account when they make their sandpaper.

Sandpaper, or "sanding media," is made by gluing tiny pieces of sharp stone, called grit, to the backings of regular paper, waterproof paper, mylar film, pressed fiber, or cloth. Most sandpapers designed for sanding bare wood use paper backings. Waterproof paper is used to back wet/dry paper, and film backing is sometimes used with very fine grit. Fiber and cloth are used for discs and belts on power sanding machines, which may also use film and paper.

Aluminum oxide is best for most raw wood sanding because it is sharp, economical, and friable. "Friable" means it fractures during use, presenting a new, sharp surface to the wood each time it cracks. It continues to sand efficiently, leaving small v-shaped scratches until it is spent.

Garnet grit starts out sharp, but it's not friable and dulls during use. I like it for final raw wood sanding because it leaves softer u-shaped scratches that tend to stain more evenly. Sanding the end grain on wood with dull garnet burnishes it, making the grain less prone to absorbing excess stain.

Silicone carbide is sharp but harder than the other two media, so it is used for sanding coats of finish (which are usually harder than wood). You could use silicone carbide paper for raw wood, but it is more expensive.

Ceramic grit is very tough, somewhat cube-shaped, and is usually used on belts and discs for machine sanding. It wears very slowly but requires more energy to abrade material.

Before staining, the upper portion was sanded with 150-grit garnet paper, the lower with 150-grit aluminum oxide.

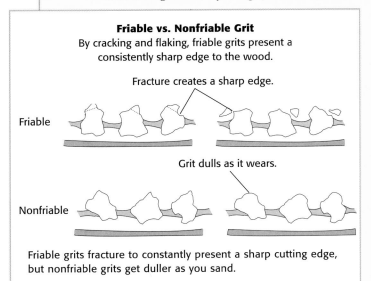

Friable vs. Nonfriable Grit
By cracking and flaking, friable grits present a consistently sharp edge to the wood.

Fracture creates a sharp edge.

Friable

Grit dulls as it wears.

Nonfriable

Friable grits fracture to constantly present a sharp cutting edge, but nonfriable grits get duller as you sand.

Both 1200- and 600-grit sandpaper feel the same to me. Is the sandpaper mislabeled, or is my sense of touch out of whack?

Manufacturers use several different grading systems to size grit, so one type of 1200 (FEPA system) is equal to another type of 600 (CAMI or ANSI system).

Sandpaper grit is graded by size. Usually higher numbers indicate a finer grit. More than one grading system is used, however. The CAMI or ANSI system uses straight numbers (80, 120, 600, etc.), while the European FEPA system uses the same numbers, but with a "P" in front (P80, P120, P600, etc.). A third system, called micron grading, reverses the order, using larger numbers for coarser grits.

To further complicate things, in the two most common systems, (CAMI/ANSI and FEPA), the grits are identical from 220 down, but differentiate as the numbers increase. Look at the chart below and you'll see that 600 CAMI/ANSI is equal to P1200 on the FEPA scale.

ABRASIVE GRADING SYSTEMS			
CAMI (ANSI)	FEPA	MIXTURE	GRADE
1500		3	RELCO FINE
		5	
		6	
1200			
		9	
1000			
800			ULTRA FINE
		15	
600	P1200		
500	P1000		
		20	
400	P800		SUPER FINE
360	P600		
		30	
	P500		
320	P400	39	EXTRA FINE
		28	
	P320		
280		45	
		50	
240	P280		VERY FINE
		50	
		60	
220	P220		
180	P180		
150	P150		
120	P125		FINE
100	P105		
80	P90		MEDIUM
60	P80		
50	P50		COARSE
40	P40		
35	P25		EXTRA COARSE

When sanding between coats, how do I judge whether or not I'm in danger of sanding through the finish?

"Good judgment comes from experience, and experience—well, that comes from poor judgment."

—Cousin Woodman

One of my favorite stories is about the woman who gets on a bus in an unfamiliar city. She sits down next to a man reading the paper. He has that air of one who is all too familiar with his daily commute.

"Excuse me," she says, "but this is my first time on this bus line and I don't know the stops. I need to get off at Elm Street. Can you help me?"

"Sure!" replies the man. "Just watch me and get off at the stop before I do."

Sanding is like that. There's no better way to learn when to stop sanding than to sand through the finish a few times, and it's not a big deal. It's only finish . . . nobody died.

Want to avoid sanding through the finish? That's one of those situations where experience is the best teacher.

Do I need to sand between coats when I'm finishing?

You don't have to sand between coats unless you need to remove finish irregularities or flatten the surface.

If it has been less than two weeks since the last coat was applied, there's no need to sand between coats. However, you should lightly sand with 320-grit paper if you've let it sit longer than that. On the other hand, you should sand between coats if there are rough spots, brush marks, orange peel, overspray, or bits of dust in the finish. Use the finest grit that will level the surface, leaving it smooth enough for the next coat.

You only need to sand between coats of finish if you must flatten irregularities or remove rough spots.

I've built a bookcase using veneered plywood that feels quite smooth as it is. Do I need to sand it before finishing?

If there is any solid wood in the piece, it's a good idea to sand even smooth veneered plywood before finishing.

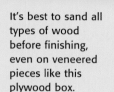

All parts of a piece must be sanded identically using the same type and size of grit. Since you'll need to sand the solid wood, you must sand the veneered parts as well. If you don't, there's a good chance that stain won't color evenly and finish won't behave the same way. Perhaps you can omit the coarsest grit on the veneer and start at 120- or even 180- grit, but be sure you complete all the pieces with the same grit. Veneer gets pressed during production, and the compressed surface can make stains and finish act unpredictably.

It's best to sand all types of wood before finishing, even on veneered pieces like this plywood box.

Some people say that smoothing the surface with a hand scraper is better than sanding. Is that true?

No, but it's okay to use any final prep method you like, providing that you do the same thing to all parts of the furniture.

Scraping can be faster than sanding. If you are skilled with a scraper, you may even get a smoother surface. But that's not necessarily an advantage when it comes to finishing. Sometimes it is okay to have some fine scratches in which pigment can lodge.

Although it is quite legitimate to scrape a piece smooth instead of sanding, remember that you must treat all parts of the the entire piece exactly the same or the finish will look different from section to section. That means that if you scrape, you must scrape the entire surface, not scrape the easy areas and sand the others. Scraping may be easy on a flat tabletop, but impractical on fluted turned legs.

Whether you sand or scrape, make sure you do exactly the same thing to all parts of the piece.

Q

What is pore filler and where do I buy it? I don't recall seeing it at the local home improvement store.

A

Pore filler is a paste made with inert material designed to fill up the pores in wood. You'll find it at woodworking specialty stores.

Some woods have large, open pores, and it is a fool's errand to try to fill them with finish. It's best to either leave them open or fill them with pore filler.

Think of pore filler as a mud slurry. Most fillers contain ground sand, talc, wood dust, or some combination of solid particles suspended in a binder, which helps the materials stick together and to the wood to which they're applied. When you apply it to a surface, the slurry fills up the pores with an inert mass that will not shrink once it is dry and cured. With the pores level to the surrounding wood, you can apply thin coats of clear or colored finish, and the surface looks smooth.

Fillers come in oil-based and water-based versions. Both work well, but water-based filler dries much faster and is easier to use than oil-based filler. Fillers are not usually sold at home improvement or paint stores, but you will find them in woodworking specialty stores and catalogs.

Q

What's the difference between pore filler and putty? Aren't both products used to fill voids in wood?

A

Both pore filler and putty fill wood, but putty is thicker and designed for larger voids.

If you look at the list of ingredients, you'd be hard-pressed to tell pore filler and putty apart. Pore filler is thinner and slower-drying than putty and is easily manipulated into small wood pores. In a pinch, you could thin your favorite putty and use it as pore filler. One brand, called Wunderfil, is sold as a putty with instructions on how to thin it for use as filler.

Pore filler (right) is similar to putty. In fact, Rockler sells a putty called Wunderfil that you can convert into pore filler by thinning with water.

Q I understand that I don't have to use pore filler for every finishing job, but when must I use it?

Pore filler is always optional, so there is never a time when you absolutely must use it. However, it is a boon when you are trying to achieve a glass-smooth finish on open-pore woods.

Pore filler is optional. Some woodworkers never use it, preferring instead to leave open-pore woods natural by keeping pores visible. Others feel that wood looks best when the surface is glass-smooth. This is especially true if you are using a high-gloss or solid-color finish. Open pores may look natural on a thin, woody, satin finish, but under high-gloss or solid colors, they just look like mistakes. Pore filler will quickly give you a glass-smooth surface that won't shrink over time.

Some woods have small pores that never require pore filler, even if you want a smooth, high-gloss finish. Small-pore woods include maple, birch, cherry, boxwood, hornbeam, holly, basswood, and virtually all softwoods.

Other woods have large, obvious pores and may benefit from pore filler. Those woods include oak, ash, mahogany, walnut, rosewood, koa, teak, and a wealth of others.

You can also use the clear finish by itself to fill up pores. By applying many coats and sanding each one until the surface is level, you will eventually fill up the pores with the clear coating. However, this takes a long time and a lot of sanding. Another disadvantage is that as the finish shrinks over time, it will sink into the pores and the pores will start to show up again. Pore filler is inert once it cures and will not shrink.

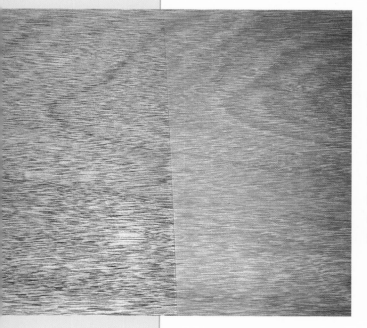

You can see the difference between "open-pore" (left) and "closed-pore" (right) finishes. The right side has pore filler below the lacquer.

Should I use pore filler on the raw wood before the stain, after the stain, or after the wood is sealed?

The rule is to fill wood after dye but before pigment. I always seal the wood prior to filler.

Dye stains are used only on raw wood, so if you are using a dye stain, apply it first. When it is dry, seal the wood with one thin coat of dewaxed shellac or Zinsser SealCoat to lock in the dye and prepare the wood for filler. Then apply the grain filler.

If you are using a pigmented stain or an off-the-shelf commercial stain, it is best to apply it after you use pore filler. Again, seal the wood first with a thin coat of dewaxed shellac or SealCoat, then apply the filler. Let it dry, lightly sand with 320-grit paper to remove any surface residue, then stain with the commercial or pigmented stain prior to the second sealer coat.

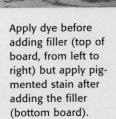

Apply dye before adding filler (top of board, from left to right) but apply pigmented stain after adding the filler (bottom board).

Should the pore filler be the same color as the wood?

The color of pore filler you chose is a matter of personal taste, but contrasting the color to the wood adds character.

It is up to you whether you want to match the pore filler to the average wood tone, or use a different color to add contrast. When the filler is the same color as the wood, the surface looks monochromatic. If that is the look you are seeking, then go for it. On the other hand, using a filler that is substantially darker or lighter than the surrounding wood adds character and more contrast to your piece.

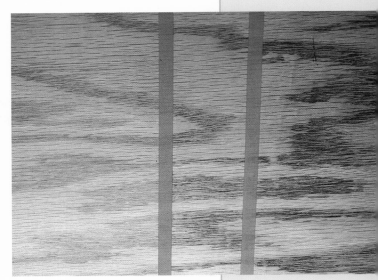

Oak panel with matching filler on the left and contrasting filler on the right. Whichever style you choose is a matter of personal taste.

Q I bought oil-based pore filler at a woodworking store. How do I use it?

A Smear the oil-based filler onto sealed wood, pack it into the pores with burlap, then rub it off across the grain as it starts to dry. After three days, sand lightly to remove the chalky residue.

This is a messy job, so set aside plenty of time and wear an apron, old clothes, and vinyl gloves. Gather all of your gear before you start. Grab some fine nylon abrasive pads or a brush, a pan for mixing the filler, mineral spirits, and a mess of clean burlap.

Seal the wood with one thin coat of Zinsser SealCoat or dewaxed shellac and let it dry for at least two hours. Pour some filler into a pan and thin it with mineral spirits until it is the consistency of light cream or half-and-half. Don the gloves and dip a piece of nylon pad, or the brush, into the filler. Scrub some filler onto an area of the sealed wood. If it is a large surface, apply filler to only one 4-ft.-square area at a time.

Let the filler dry partway, just until it loses its wet look and starts turning dusky. While it is still the consistency of mud, pack the filler into the pores by rubbing it in with burlap. Before it dries completely, remove the excess by rubbing across the grain with a clean piece of burlap. Let the filler dry for three days, then lightly sand the surface with 320-grit paper to remove the chalky residue. Seal it with another coat of SealCoat or dewaxed shellac before finishing.

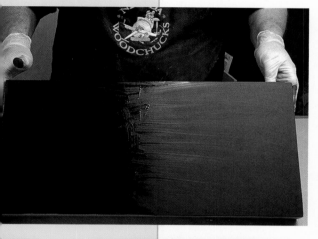

Freshly applied filler looks wet (left side) but will soon dry to a dusky haze (right side).

Once the filler becomes hazy, use burlap to remove the excess filler by scrubbing across the grain.

Is the technique different for applying water-based filler and oil-based filler?

Applying water-based filler is easy. Brush or rub the filler on and immediately squeegee it off. Let it dry a few hours, then sand lightly.

Water-based pore filler dries much faster than oil-based filler, and there is no need to pack it into the pores. Start by sealing the wood with one thin coat of Zinsser SealCoat or dewaxed shellac and let it dry for at least two hours.

Most water-based fillers come ready to use and do not require thinning, but you do need to stir them well. Use either a synthetic bristle brush or a nylon abrasive pad to apply the filler liberally to the sealed wood, taking care to scrub it into the pores. As soon as you are done applying it, use a credit card or a piece of plastic laminate with a smooth edge to squeegee it off. This will push the filler into the pores and remove the excess. Let it dry for several hours, then sand off any chalky residue on the surface with 320-grit paper. Seal the dry filler with another thin coat of SealCoat.

Spread water-based filler evenly on the surface of your project, then immediately squeegee off the excess with a credit card or a scrap of plastic laminate.

What do I use to custom-color pore filler?

Universal tinting colors will work for all filler. Or use Japan colors for oil-based filler and acrylics for water-based filler.

Tint oil-based filler by adding Japan colors or artist's oil colors, both of which are concentrated pigment pastes. Universal tinting color pastes, available from some woodworking specialty stores, work with both oil- and water-based fillers. For water-based filler, use artist's acrylic colors or the acrylic paints from your local craft store. Don't use furniture stains for either, because they are too thin and lack sufficient pigment density.

Tint oil-based filler with Japan or oil colors (left). Tint water-based filler with artist acrylics (right). Universal tinting colors (center) work with both types of filler.

Q What sort of putty should I buy and how do I use it? What if I can't find the right color?

A Most brands of putty work well. Choose a color that matches the wood or custom-color it yourself. Filling gouges is as easy as pressing putty into the void, waiting for it to dry, and sanding flush to the wood.

Test the putty with your thumbnail. If it leaves an impression, it is not yet dry enough to sand.

There are many quick-drying solvent-based and water-based putties in a selection of common colors. Most are ready to use, but a few are sold as powders ready to mix with water. All of them work well for the normal dings and gouges you find on interior furniture and millwork. There are even special putties designed for exterior use, including a UV-curing version that hardens in sunlight.

If you can't find exactly the color you need, there are two options. The easiest is to mix two or three different colors of the same brand and type of putty. Otherwise, choose a light-colored putty and modify it with pigment pastes. Use artist's oil colors for oil-based putty and artist's acrylics for water-based putty. If you have them, universal tinting colors will work for either type, but you'll only find them at wood specialty stores.

Use a putty knife to press the putty into the void, leaving it just slightly proud of the surrounding surface. That way you'll still be able to sand it flush to the wood even if it shrinks during drying, which most putties tend to do. Check to see if the putty is ready to sand by pressing your thumbnail into the center of it. If it is soft enough to leave a nail impression, wait a bit longer. Then, use a sanding block to level the fill so it stays flat.

Q **E**very time I try to repair a broken corner by building it up with putty, it crumbles off. What am I doing wrong?

A *You'll need something a bit stronger than normal putty to repair a broken corner. Use colored epoxy or polyester auto body fill and anchor it with wire brads.*

Very large voids, loose knots, or repairs of an exposed edge require a certain technique using putty. First, drive a few brads into the edge of the problem area to act as anchors. Make sure they don't protrude past the edges of where the wood was before it was damaged. Mix epoxy with wood dust or colored pigment powders and use it to fill the void. Build a dam of masking tape to help shape it. Overfill the void, leaving the filler slightly proud so that you can sand it flush to the wood once it cures. Colored epoxy also works well for filling loose knots, since it glues the knot in as it fills the void around it.

Some companies, such as System III and Gougeon Bros., offer thin epoxies that can be mixed with fillers. They also sell several different types of filler that will change the epoxy from thin and runny to the consistency of mashed potatoes, or anything in between. You'll also find epoxy putty, which is great for molding missing or damaged parts and still strong enough to do the job.

If you are working on a piece that will be painted a solid color, you can do this same trick with a polyester auto body filler, such as Bondo. As before, add brads as anchors, build a masking tape dam, and drop in the filler after it is mixed. Set it into place and use a toothpick to jiggle out any air bubbles before the polyester sets.

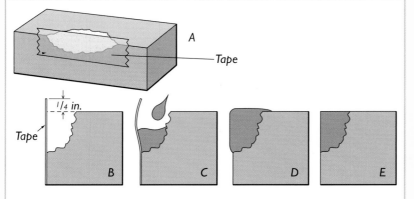

Make a dam of masking tape to hold the epoxy in place while it cures.

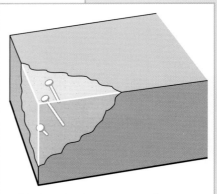

Add a few brads to act as anchors before you cast putty for a corner repair.

Do I need to use primer before I paint? Which one should I use?

It is always wise, and almost always necessary, to use primer before painting. Different primers are good for different jobs, but water-based primers are a good default choice.

Primer, which is simply an opaque sealer, prepares a surface for paint. That's true whether you are painting over raw wood for the first time or going over an existing paint or clear finish. Primer does a better job of sticking to any substrate, painted or raw, than does paint. It will also seal in any contamination, and create a good bonding surface for the next coat. Curiously, any type of paint sticks to any type of primer, so don't hesitate to put oil-based paint over water-based primer or vice versa.

Water-based primers are the most common ones with the widest range of applications. They are typically designed for both indoor and outdoor use, and for priming everything from exterior wood siding to interior furniture, moldings, and walls. Water-based primer is a must for bathrooms and a wise choice whenever you are unsure what to use.

To hide tough stains, watermarks, odors, or simply when you want a faster-drying material, Zinsser makes an alcohol-based primer called BIN. It is popular with cabinetmakers and finish carpenters who prize it because it dries fast, sands easily, and sticks to virtually anything. However, it is only for interior use.

Certain types of stains, such as tannin and nicotine, will bleed through water-based primers. Oil-based primer is the best choice for these situations, whether they occur indoors or out. Though oil-based primers are becoming increasingly less common, Zinsser still makes one called CoverStain.

Your local paint store will have a variety of special primers to cover every need.

Q What is sanding sealer? When do I need to use it?

Sanding sealer is optional on most woods. But it can help save time when finishing absorbent woods because it is easy to sand and seals more effectively than lacquer.

Originally, the need for sanding sealer arose from a problem with spray lacquer, which became popular during the early part of the 20th century. When you spray nitrocellulose lacquer onto a fairly absorbent wood such as pine, poplar, or gumwood, it seems as if the first few coats are completely absorbed by the wood, leaving the surface dry. Another problem with lacquer is that it is fairly difficult to sand.

Manufacturers created sanding sealer by adding stearates to the lacquer. Stearates are soft, fluffy, soap-like additives that give lacquer more loft to quickly fill the small pores of absorbent woods. In addition, stearates make the lacquer film much softer and they act as a lubricant, two qualities that make the sealer substantially easier to sand. That's where we get the name sanding sealer. You'll find many iterations of sanding sealer. Some are multiple-use and act as contamination sealers as well. Others are wide-spectrum sealers used for topcoats other than lacquer. You will find at least one product labeled sanding sealer that contains no stearates.

Use sanding sealer under lacquer or to make the first sanding on absorbent woods easier. But don't overuse it. Covering a thick coat of soft sanding sealer with lacquer can cause the lacquer to prematurely chip or crack. If you use sanding sealer, limit it to one or two coats to help maintain the clarity of your finish. The stearates in sanding sealer make it slightly cloudy when it is applied too thickly.

Sanding sealer is lacquer that is laced with stearates that powder and lubricate the surface to make sanding easier.

The stearates in sanding sealer (right) make it look cloudy compared to clear lacquer (left).

Q **I use a variety of finishes, and I am never sure which sealer goes with which finish. Can you pair them up for me?**

A *SealCoat or dewaxed shellac will go under any finish. However, not all finishes require a sealer.*

Zinsser SealCoat, which is a wax-free shellac, is the universal sealer that will go over any wood and under any finish and is always a safe default choice. It is especially good for sealing in contamination problems and for making any stain compatible with any coating. Water-based coatings, for example, often have a hard time sticking to oil-based stains, but SealCoat will make them work together.

However, not all coatings require sealers. Shellac, Danish oil, and all oil-based polyurethanes and varnishes are self-sealing and don't need more sealer. That's not to say you can't use one—you can—but it is not necessary.

On the other hand, it is always wise to use a sealer under lacquer and all water-based coatings.

Q **The end grain of solid wood pieces always seems to suck up too much stain and finish. Is there some way to seal it first?**

A *The three ways to deal with end-grain problems are sanding, sealing, and sizing.*

Presealing the end grain with SealCoat (right side of board) will prevent it from absorbing too much stain.

First, try sanding the end grain with worn garnet paper, which dulls as you use it. That will burnish the wood and reduce stain absorption. If that's not enough, seal the end grain before you finish or stain. Use dewaxed shellac or Zinsser SealCoat. Flood it on, then wipe off everything that has not been absorbed. An alternative method is to brush the end grain with a coat of glue size made of hide glue thinned 50/50 with water.

Q **I run across so many problems when I seal furniture or interior millwork. Which sealers will solve these problems?**

- **Bleeding pitch in pine**
- **Problem woods like rosewood and cedar**
- **Cat urine on hardwood floors**
- **Smoke smell, musty odors**
- **Grease, dirt, wax**

A *You can seal in all of the above with Zinsser SealCoat or fresh dewaxed shellac, or for pieces that will be painted, use Zinsser BIN. One coat will usually do, but in extreme cases use two coats.*

For other, more complex problems, here's what I'd do:

• *Silicone contamination* (contributes to fisheye)

The first step is to eliminate as much of the silicone oil on the surface as possible, then seal in whatever cannot be removed. Silicone usually shows up on pieces that are being refinished. After stripping the finish, scrub the raw wood with copious amounts of mineral spirits. This is the solvent for silicone oil and will create a mixture of mineral spirits and dissolved silicone oil. Mop up as much of the liquid as possible while it is wet. Follow by scrubbing the piece with a mixture of ¼ cup ammonia in a quart of warm water. Mop up as much as possible, then rinse with plenty of clean water. Let the piece dry overnight, sand very lightly with 320-grit paper to remove the raised whiskers on the wood, then seal the wood with one or two coats of Zinsser SealCoat or fresh dewaxed shellac.

• *Nicotine stains under paint*

Most water-based and alcohol-based sealers are not particularly effective in blocking out nicotine stains. The ideal choice for that job is an oil-based sealer. Zinsser CoverStain, in my opinion, is the best of the lot.

SealCoat, a wax-free shellac mixture, will even seal in cat urine odors.

Application Tools and Methods

Q How do I avoid drips and runs when I finish a vertical surface?

A *Prefinish, lay the piece down, or use wipe-on finishing techniques.*

Drips are the bane of a finisher's existence. There are several strategies—short of becoming a flawless practitioner of this black art—that will help eliminate runs. The first is prefinishing. Since the parts are usually fairly small prior to assembly, you'll be able to avoid drips, runs, and sags by setting them horizontally to work on.

But even items that cannot be prefinished can often still be finished horizontally. Don't be afraid to lay a cabinet down on sawhorses and brush or spray one side at a time. Turn it to do the next side only after the finish has set up so that it no longer sags or runs. It may mean a longer time allotted for your finishing schedule, but you'll get better results. In rare cases where you can't lay the piece down but you can move it, turn the piece upside down. Runs show because they created a shadow below the bead of the drip. That shadow disappears once you turn the piece right side up again, and the sag or drip becomes almost invisible.

Consider the convenient option of a wipe-on finish when you absolutely must finish right side up and assembled. Most coatings can be wiped on and off with little or no modification, and if you do so, there won't be enough material on the surface to drip or run. Polyurethane gel, which neither sags nor runs, has become a popular option, possibly for this reason alone.

Whenever possible, lay bookcases or case goods on their sides on blocks or horses for drip-free finishing.

Although liquid polyurethane drips and runs (right side of board), polyurethane gel (left) does not, even when thickly applied.

Q Masking tapes seem to come in many colors and prices. Are there really any differences, or should I just buy the cheapest?

There really are differences from one tape to another. Bite the bullet and pay for specialty tapes when you need them. You'll be glad you did.

Regular beige masking tape is not appropriate for stopping finish from bleeding under a line. Stains and finishes tend to creep underneath and dissolve the

adhesive. If the tape it is left on too long, it will tear and leave adhesive residue on the wood. Fortunately, there are alternatives. The 3M Company color-codes their tapes to make identification easier. For example, 3M's bright green lacquer tape is impervious to most stain and finish solvents, and is waterproof, as well. It should be removed in a day or two, but it will give you a crisp line with no adhesive residue.

Bright blue painter's tape can be left on for a week (and sometimes longer) and still come off clean without tearing or leaving adhesive residue. This is the best choice for prefinishing, or any situation where you must leave the tape on for a long time. I find this a great all-around tape, and it's the one I reach for most often in my shop.

From top to bottom, flexible fine-line tape (olive), masking tape (tan), lacquer tape (green), low-tack paper tape (white), and painter's tape (blue).

Automotive pinstriping tape is a flexible, semitransparent, light green tape. Unlike other tapes, which are made of paper or cloth, pinstriping tape has a flexible film backing. This allows it to stretch sideways so that you can mask curved lines without wrinkling the tape. For delicate surfaces, buy white, low-tack, paper-backed tape designed to come off without pulling up wallpaper or old finishes.

Masking tape (right) may tear when left on too long. Blue painter's tape (left) will lift off cleanly.

Tape often tears and pulls up slivers of wood when I try to remove it from a masked line. What am I doing wrong?

You do need to use the right type of tape for the job. But there is a way to encourage tape to come off easily. Pull the tape back over itself and away from the clean edge at about a 30-degree angle.

On thick finishes, lightly cut the finish along the edge of the tape with a razor blade before removing it.

No matter how deft you are at removing it, the wrong tape will leave glue residue and will tear if left on too long. Use bright green lacquer tape or pinstriper's tape to achieve crisp definition lines between colors. Choose blue painter's tape if it will be left in place for more than a day or two. Even after you have chosen the right tape, there is a right way (and many wrong ways) to remove it.

Yanking tape upward is one of the wrong ways. That will tear the tape, pull up wood fibers, and cause chips of finish to come up with the tape if it is next to a finished edge. The result is a jagged edge where the coating ends. The correct way to take up tape is to lift one corner and pull it back over itself. Keep the back of the tape as close to the surface of the wood as possible. Pull the tape at about a 30- degree angle away from the finished edge. This will give you a clean crisp line where the finish ends.

With very thick finishes, you may have to score the finish first with a razor blade before removing the tape.

Pull the tape back over itself and away from the painted edge at about 30 degrees.

Is there a simple way to mask when I use two colors on one piece, or when I work on a piece with curves and odd-shaped cutouts?

For complex masking jobs, use sheets of clear, self-adhesive book-cover plastic. Cut out the shape, press it on, and remove it when the paint is set.

Not long ago a friend of mine painted a cylinder to look as if the entire outer surface had one color of paint cascading down it in irregular sheets over a second color. I've painted boxes with a pattern of exposed shapes created by using a sponge technique. The patterns on both pieces were achieved by masking the surfaces with sheets of clear vinyl.

Visit the local craft store or office supply outlet, and you'll find pressure-sensitive-adhesive(PSA)-backed vinyl designed to be used as protective book-cover material. PSA means it will have a peel-and-stick backing; the particular adhesive on this type of vinyl peels off easily without leaving a residue. It won't damage the finish or wood beneath it, and it forms a clean edge when used to mask most finishes. Bookcover sheets come in a variety of colors and patterns, but I prefer working with clear vinyl so I can see what I am masking.

Cut a mask out of clear, self-adhesive book-cover plastic to cover irregular or difficult shapes before painting.

To work with PSA-backed vinyl, use scissors or a razor knife to cut out the desired shapes while the paper backing is still intact. First, lay it in place for alignment, then peel off the protective backing and press the mask onto the wood. Spray, brush, wipe, or stipple the color on, then peel off the mask as soon as the paint is set. Don't wait until the paint is completely dry, or the vinyl may peel the paint with it as it's removed.

Q

What are the best brushes for solvent- or oil-based coatings like shellac, lacquer, varnish, and polyurethane?

Without question, I prefer to use natural-bristle brushes such as China (hog) bristle for oil-based coatings, and ox hair, fitch, or blends for shellac and lacquer.

A natural-bristle brush is best for working with these finishes. Bristle brushes are made from the hair (bristles) of various animals. Try as we might, we have never topped nature's ability to make fine hair with just the right give and spring for applying finish.

Characteristics of springiness and softness vary in animal-hair brushes, and therefore they are best paired with certain finishes. For fairly heavy-bodied coatings, like oil-based polyurethane, varnish, and paint, I like the springy quality of China bristles. China bristle is hair from a particular Chinese hog. Colors vary from white through brown, gray, and black. In nature, white hair is slightly softer, but color may not be a valid indicator, since the bristles are often dyed.

Both fitch, from a relative of our skunk, and ox hair are much softer and leave fewer brush marks in very thin finishes. Either bristle works well with shellac and lacquer. More common and perhaps better is a blend of these types of hair with China bristle. Blended brushes give you the best qualities of two or more types of hair.

For most cabinet work, use a 2-in. or 3-in. brush—whichever is more comfortable in your hand. Jump to a 3-in. or 4-in. brush for large surfaces, such as the exterior of your house or a large panel. Keep one or two 1-in. sash brushes with angled ends for small areas and for cutting into tight corners, such as the fields on raised-panel doors.

I prefer these ox-hair and hog-bristle-blend brushes for shellac, lacquer, and thin varnishes.

An angled sash brush easily gets into the inside corners of this tray.

Q What's the best type of brush to use with water-based coatings?

A nylon brush works well with water-based coatings, but a paint pad will work better on flat surfaces. A natural-bristle brush does not work well with a water-based finish.

Natural bristles tend to splay and lose their spring when wet, so they are not good choices for water-based coatings. Any synthetic bristle brush will work, including polyester, nylon, and an assortment of blends with trade names, such as Nylox, Chinex, and Taklon.

Sometimes the best brush is a pad. These paint pads work well with all water-based coatings, including paints.

Brush marks often occur when you use water-based coatings because they dry fast. The stiff bristle ends tend to flip through the coating creating air bubbles, a problem known as "foaming." Nylon and other soft blends leave fewer brush marks than stiffer synthetics and are also less prone to foaming. Though you shouldn't use natural brushes with water-based coatings, you can use synthetics for oil-based finishes.

Sometimes the best brush for a water-based coating is not a brush at all but a paint pad. Think of a paint pad as a huge brush with thousands of extremely short bristles spread out over a large surface. Paint pads alleviate the three most common water-based application problems: foaming, applying too much coating at once, and failure to keep a wet edge.

The soft nap of a paint pad reduces brush marks and minimizes foaming because the bristles are too short to whisk through the finish. Its large surface makes it easier to apply a sufficiently thin coat of finish to a wide swath of wood. By covering a wide area of wood quickly, the pad lets you apply the next pass while the first still has a wet edge. Each adjacent stroke flows into the previous one, resulting in a smoother finish. Unfortunately, a pad only works on fairly flat surfaces. For carvings, fluted columns, and the like, you'll still need a brush.

Q **What are the characteristics of a quality brush?**

Quality brushes are higher in price, have plenty of long bristles, a clean, uniform chisel-shaped end, and bristles that won't pull out when you tug on them.

"You get what you pay for" is a true adage when it comes to buying a brush. Bargain brushes are usually inexpensive, but they are no bargain. They generally carry less finish and leave brush marks and bristles in your coating. Bite the bullet and be prepared to pay $25 and up for a good 2½-in. China-bristle brush, and even more for ox-hair blends. They're worth it.

Choose a brush that is comfortable in your hand and looks well-made. I prefer a wood handle set securely into a copper or stainless-steel ferrule. Bristles should be densely packed and sufficiently long. A 2½-in. brush, for example, should have bristles that are stacked about ⅝-in. thick and at least 2¾-in. long. For clear finishes, choose a brush with a chisel shape. The bristles should not come out if you tug lightly on them. Deflect the bristles against your hand and release them to see how they snap back. They should feel fairly soft and supple, but still springy. Press the end onto a flat surface and deflect the bristles about 45 degrees. The end of the brush should form a clean, straight line, and the ends of the bristles should ramp gently down to the surface of the wood.

My favorite varnish brush is a Sprig model made by Purdy. It has a chisel end, 2½-in. black China bristles on a wooden beavertail-shaped handle, and a stainless-steel ferrule. The bristles are 2⅞-in. long and ⅝-in. thick.

A quality brush (left) should have long, firmly set bristles that form a clean, straight line when deflected.

Wood plugs inside the metal ferrule create spaces, called the reservoir, in the brush. Bristles are set in tapered ranks.

Q **Is a varnish brush the same thing as a paintbrush?**

A *Varnish- and paintbrushes are different. You can use a varnish brush for paint, but you shouldn't use a paint brush for varnish.*

The difference between a varnish brush and a paint brush is in the shape of the bristle ends. Varnish brushes are chisel shaped, while paint brushes are usually cut straight across. The chisel shape allows the bristles to taper to the wood in a gentle ramp. Straight-cut bristles end abruptly. Chisel ends leave fewer brush marks. This is less critical when using paint, which does not show brush marks as easily, but I prefer to use chisel-end brushes for painting as well. By the way, sash brushes, which are angled, are made with both chisel- and flat-cut ends. Use the chisel-end variety.

Q **Is a foam brush as good as a natural-bristle brush for varnish and polyurethane?**

A *Though a foam brush won't work as well with a finish as a natural-bristle brush does, many people prefer to use foam, with successful results.*

A gray "foam-wedge-on-a-stick" brush is fine for applying stain or first coats, but I would not use this variety of brush for quality varnish work. Bristles, both natural and synthetic, hold more coating per stroke, which allows you to blend wet edges more easily. They also conform to any shape. If you ever try coating flutes, carvings, or edge moldings with an inflexible foam brush, you'll see what I mean.

On the plus side, foam brushes are inexpensive enough to throw away without cleaning, and many finishers swear by them. Where the quality of coating isn't critical, such as in applying stain or a flood coat that will be wiped off, foam is a good choice. However, avoid foam when using shellac or lacquer. They contain solvents that will destroy the foam brush.

bristles
reservoir
divider
setting
ferrule
handle

varnish brush   paint brush

Varnish brushes (left) have chisel-shaped ends. Paint-brush ends are cut straight.

Foam-on-a-stick brushes won't cut it for quality varnish work, but they are fine for throwaway jobs like staining.

Q What's the right way to clean a brush?

Rejuvenate a brush as you work with it, and cleaning will be easy. To clean, use a solvent wash, then soapy water. Rinse the brush and set the shape for it to dry.

Treating a brush well while you work is key. So before you dip a brush into oil, polyurethane, or varnish, soak the bristles all the way to the ferrule in mineral spirits.

Use water for water-based, alcohol for shellac, and lacquer thinner for lacquer. This wets the bristles and loads the reservoir, helping the finish flow. Squeeze out all excess solvent, leaving the bristles wet, but not sopping wet. Dip only the last third or half of the bristles into the coating. The upper ends should be wet with solvent, not loaded with coating.

As you work, finish will creep up toward the ferrule and start to dry. Before a crust forms, stop and clean the brush by massaging the bristles in a pan of the appropriate solvent. Squeeze out the solvent and go back to work. This process will take about 10 seconds for every 10 minutes or so of brushing and will leave the brush clean and wet, just as when you started.

When you are finished, scrape off any excess finish on the edge of the can or brush it out onto newspaper. Once again, clean the bristles in solvent by massaging or using a brush comb. Get them as clean as you can, then squeeze out the excess solvent, but leave the bristles wet. Take the brush to the sink and wash it several times with plenty of warm water and dish soap or shampoo. Rinse out all the soap, then spin the brush to remove some of the water.

Finally, set the bristles by wrapping the damp brush in brown-bag paper. Feel for the ends of the bristles, and fold the paper over about 1 in. past the ends. This will reshape the brush as it dries. This entire process will keep your brushes in good shape so you can use them over and over again.

After rinsing in solvent, wash the brush thoroughly with soap and water. Rinse completely and spin the brush to remove most of the water.

Wrap the still-wet bristles in brown-bag paper. Feel for the ends. Fold the bag 1 in. past the ends.

Q **Is it correct to hold a brush by its handle?**

You should hold a brush by the ferrule for better control and comfort. The handle is used mostly while cleaning the brush.

Just as you learned to hold a pen or pencil a certain way, there is an ideal, ergonomic way to hold a brush that gives you maximum control and prevents hand cramps and fatigue.

Granted, anything that works for you is fine with me, but at least give this a try before you settle on your own style. Lay the handle in the crook of your hand so that it goes between your thumb and first finger. Grab the ferrule with your fingers straight and relaxed on one side, and your thumb opposing them. The bristles should now look and act like an extension of your fingers. If you can comfortably run your fingertips over a surface, you can control the brush bristles on it, as well.

Hold the brush by grasping it by the ferrule with the handle in the crook between your thumb and first finger.

This Syntox brush by Purdy uses a new type of bristle that works with both water- and oil-based coatings.

Q **Is there one type of brush I can use for shellac, oil varnish, and water-based paints?**

Years ago, I would have said that you need a whole range of brushes, but today, there are synthetic bristle brushes good enough for all these finishing applications.

Brush manufacturers are working with companies that make synthetic fibers to create bristles that act like natural fibers, but are not subject to water problems. Such a brush would perform like a fine, natural-hair brush with oil-based, solvent-based, and water-based coatings alike. Luckily, these brushes do exist. A good example is the Syntox line of brushes made by Purdy, my favorite brush company. Syntox brushes have a combination of synthetic nylon and Chinex bristles. These brushes are a fine example of the modern brush-maker's art and will work with every coating you are likely to apply.

Q How do I brush a raised panel without getting puddles in the corners?

A To avoid puddles in corners, first address the fields with a small sash brush, follow with the panel, and then coat the frame.

I use two different brushes for finishing a raised panel. The best process is to first coat the fields and molded-frame edge, beginning about an inch away from the inside corner using a 1-in. angled sash brush. When the brush is mostly unloaded, go back and stroke the finish from the corner outward in both directions. When the recessed areas are finished, switch to a larger brush and coat the panel as you would any flat surface. Then, coat the rails, and don't worry about going over the seam line. You'll straighten out the brush marks when you get to the stiles. Angle the brush so that it fits the width of the frame, and go with the grain. Use the small sash brush to hit the edges of the door last.

Start brushing a raised-panel door with a small, angled sash brush in the corner of the field.

Q How do I eliminate bubbles in brushed finishes?

A The best way to be free of bubbles is to avoid creating them, but tipping off will help remove any that show up.

To tip off, hold the brush at 90 degrees. Drag just the tips of the bristles through the wet finish.

Good brush technique will eliminate most bubbles before they start. Scrubbing finish onto wood instead of gently laying it down will form bubbles, as will working with finish that is too thick, or trying to put too much finish at once onto wood with large pores. Vigorously shaking cans of finish can form bubbles too, so it's best to stir finishes instead of shaking them. When bubbles show up in spite of your best efforts, remove them by tipping off (see page 69).

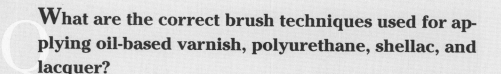

What are the correct brush techniques used for applying oil-based varnish, polyurethane, shellac, and lacquer?

There is a brush technique I prefer to use for most finishes, and it is outlined in detail below. With only slight variations, this process should work for all these finishes.

Step one: Begin by dipping only the first third of the bristles into the varnish. Touch the tips to the side of the pan.

Start by preparing the finish. Stir the finish and pour some out into a pan, preferably a square one with straight sides. Thin it for the right consistency. For most oil-based varnish or polyurethane, that means reducing it about 15 percent with mineral spirits or Penetrol. Shellac or lacquer should be no thicker than milk. Water-based finishes generally come ready to use with no thinning necessary, but if they seem too thick, add a bit of Floetrol.

Prepare the brush by wetting it up to the ferrule in the solvent for thinning your coating. Squeeze out the excess and dip only one-third to one-half the bristles into the coating to load the brush. Gently touch the tips of the bristles to the side of the pan. This will prevent drips on your way to the wood, but will not unload the brush. Don't scrape the bristles across the edge of the pan because that unloads the brush.

Brushing is a rather Zen-like activity. If you approach it in a relaxed and focused manner, it will go smoothly. Let's start with a flat panel to get up to speed. Set the tip of the brush onto the wood about an inch from one edge of the panel. Brush away from the edge, then come back after the first pass while the brush is unloaded and blend the finish toward the edge by going the other direction. If you start exactly at the edge, you'll get a drip down the adjacent side.

Hold the brush at about a 45-degree angle and deflect the bristles slightly until finish rises to

Step two: Start your stroke about an inch or so from the edge, with the brush at about 45 degrees.

their top surface. Move the brush with the grain, allowing the finish to gently slide off the brush and onto the wood. Think of it as sliding the brush out from under the finish. As you continue, deflect the bristles more to keep finish flowing. When finish stops flowing smoothly, go back to the pan and reload the brush.

When you come to the end of the panel, relieve the pressure on the brush to "undeflect" the bristles as you end your brush stroke and lift up off the wood. Flipping deflected bristles off the end of a board will fling paint where you don't want it. Lay each brush stroke next to the one before it so that the edges blend while they are still wet. Don't overlap strokes if you can avoid it. Work quickly, but calmly, and don't stop to admire your work partway through, or your wet edge will dry.

This is the part in the process where variations can occur. When brushing fast-drying finish, like shellac, lacquer, or water-based coatings, go back and tip off, as described below, immediately after each brush stroke. Tip off oil-based coatings, like varnish and polyurethane, only after you have coated one entire surface, such as a tabletop or a raised panel.

Here's how to tip off. First, unload the brush by scraping it across the edge of the pan. Hold the brush straight up and down at 90 degrees to the wood. Lightly touch just the tips of the bristles to the finish, and with the brush still at a 90-degree angle, gently drag just the very tip of the brush across the top of the wet finish. This will pick up bits of dust, break up air bubbles, and smooth brush marks.

Step three: As the stroke continues, deflect the brush to bring more finish to the top surface of the bristles.

Step four: Ease up and lift the brush at the end of the board to avoid flinging finish from the bristles.

Q **Should I buy spray equipment and will it give me a better finish?**

A *The answer to whether spray equipment is necessary is an unequivocal "maybe." If you need speed at the expense of efficiency and cost, or if spraying finish is your dream, then by all means, buy spray equipment.*

Let's start with the cold, hard truth. A good finisher can create a superb finish with or without a spray gun. The gun does not create quality. In fact, spraying is the least efficient way to apply a finish. It wastes more coating, requires more equipment, and uses more electricity than brushes, rags, rollers, or pads. On the plus side, it is the fastest method, and some might argue that it is also the most fun. The fun factor alone might make it worthwhile.

Spray coatings are designed to go on fast and dry fast. You can quickly apply more finish to a larger surface with a gun than with any other method.

Spraying is fast, but wasteful, as witnessed by the cloud of overspray bouncing off this bookcase interior.

Since spray guns can use very fast-drying coatings, your real time, or drying time, is also greatly reduced. However, even the most efficient guns waste 30 percent or more of the finish in the form of overspray, which is lacquer that either misses the wood or bounces back off it and goes into the air. The bottom line is that if you are willing to spend more on coatings, equipment, and electricity in order to save on labor and drying time, then you should buy spray equipment.

Will a gun give you a better finish? A spray gun, like a brush, chisel, plane, table saw, and lathe, is simply a tool. Some people find that a certain tool works better for them. If you really like spray guns and can make them work better than a rag or brush, it is entirely possible that you will get a better finish by spraying. But to be fair, you, not the gun, create the finish.

What is an HVLP gun and is it better to use than a conventional spray gun?

A High Volume Low Pressure (HVLP) gun is designed to use more air at lower pressures, which offers better transfer efficiency. An HVLP gun will cost more than a conventional spray gun, and depending on your situation, it may be worth the investment.

A conventional spray gun, for years the most common type of sprayer, uses compressed air at fairly high pressure. Like all spray guns, conventional ones atomize finish by forming it into tiny droplets, mixing the droplets with air, and propelling the mist in a pattern toward the wood. A conventional gun is fairly inexpensive, but must be connected to at least a small air compressor. Since mist is propelled at high speed, a good bit of coating either misses the wood or bounces back off it. The percentage that remains on the wood is described as the "transfer efficiency." A conventional gun often has a transfer efficiency in the 25 percent range, meaning only 25 percent of the finish you buy actually ends up on the wood. However, a conventional gun can tackle any finish, thick or thin.

An HVLP gun uses more air at a lower pressure to create a gentler mist of finish. It has a higher transfer efficiency—usually 65 percent or better—so it wastes less coating and creates less "overspray," the clouds of airborne finish that miss the wood. An HVLP is more expensive, but you save money in the long run.

There are two types of HVLP guns. One type is fed by a turbine and comes in a kit with the gun, turbine, and hoses. The turbine kit is expensive, and the smaller ones spray only thin finishes. They use standard 110-volt house current and are portable. Conversion HVLP, the other type of HVLP gun, converts high-pressure compressed air to a lower-pressure mist. It will spray thick or thin finish, costs more than conventional guns but less than a turbine, but it is not portable, and requires a 6-hp or larger compressor.

From left to right: Turbine-fed HVLP gun, conversion HVLP gun, and conventional gun sit before two turbine units.

Which type of spray gun should I buy, an HVLP, regular, or airless version?

Whether you buy a turbine HVLP, conversion HVLP, airless, air-assist, or a conventional gun depends upon your needs, budget, and the size of your compressor.

Each gun has its strengths and weaknesses. Turbine HVLP comes as a kit including the turbine, gun, and hoses, and generally costs over $600. The number of stages in the turbine determines what finishes it will spray. A one- or two-stage turbine will only spray thin coatings, but a three- or four-stage, which is more costly, will spray thicker ones. These self-contained rigs are portable for job-site projects.

Conversion HVLP is only a gun and must be fed air from a compressor. It is therefore not portable, but is less expensive than a turbine rig and will spray all finishes, thick or thin. If you spray in the shop and own a 6-hp or larger compressor, this is your best option. It is both more expensive and more efficient than a conventional gun. Conventional guns also use a compressor, but any size will do. These guns are the cheapest and will spray all coatings, but they waste more finish and generate more overspray. They are best for shops with a small compressor and a low equipment budget.

Airless guns use an onboard pump to atomize and project finish. These inexpensive, portable electric guns are good enough for homeowners to spray garage doors but will not provide furniture-quality atomization. These guns are not the same as the more expensive and powerful pump rigs for spraying houses, though both are called airless. Air-assist guns are a hybrid, using both compressed air and a pump to deliver high-quality spraying of any finish. They are the most expensive of the lot.

CHOOSING THE RIGHT GUN

CHART	COST	PORTABLE	SPRAY ALL COATINGS	REQUIRE COMPRESSOR
Conventional	Low	No	Yes	Yes
Turbine HVLP	High	Yes	No	No
Conv. HVLP	Med	No	Yes	Yes
Airless	Low	Yes	No	No
Air assist	High	No	Yes	Yes

Q Do I need a spray booth?

A Only if you plan to spray.

I realize that many people view a spray booth as an expensive annoyance mandated by some vague government agency, but it is really much more than that. The problem is that atomizing any finish turns it into an airborne cloud that envelops you and lands on everything else in the shop. The spray booth is designed to move that cloud away from you.

A spray booth is basically an air funnel. You stand at the wide end and spray toward the fan at the small end, which draws the air away from you and your furniture, and out of the building. A commercial booth, designed for spraying highly flammable materials, is fire-resistant metal fitted with explosion-resistant fans and lights. If you're planning on spraying lots of flammable materials, it's a good investment.

However, even garage hobby shops benefit from a simple booth. A booth does not have to be a complex or expensive affair. You can make one yourself from drywall and metal studs, pipe, and plastic sheeting, or even cardboard and duct tape, especially if you are spraying nonflammable water-based coatings. The core of a booth is a robust exhaust fan covered with filter material to prevent finish from going through the fan. The booth serves to funnel air from a wide opening through a small outlet. You need clean replacement air coming into the room also.

Commercial operations are subject to a wealth of regulations regarding spraying, exhaust fan size, and flammability issues. Hobby shops are not, but the local fire marshal and your insurance company can offer advice to keep your shop safe and legal. It would be wise to alert them to your intent to spray.

A spray booth can be a complex affair, like this explosive-proof commercial setup for spraying flammable coatings . . .

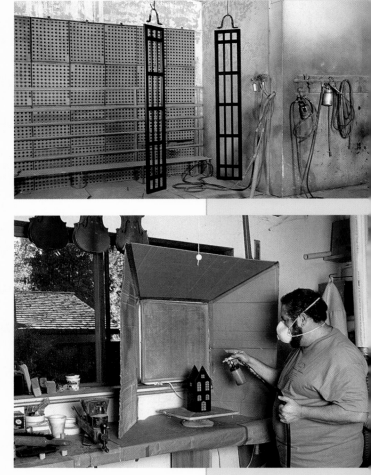

Or something as simple as this cardboard funnel on a window fan for spraying water-based materials.

Q How do I adjust my new spray gun so that it sprays correctly?

A Read the gun's literature to learn how to adjust the gun mechanisms, and test the spray pattern on cardboard before spraying furniture.

Before you start to spray, adjust the controls of the gun and learn how they work. Fill the gun with water, solvent, or finish, and prop up a good-sized piece of scrap cardboard. Hold the gun parallel to the cardboard with the tip about 8 in. away from the surface. Pull the trigger and quickly release it. You should have either a round shape, or a uniform elongated oval spray pattern. If the pattern is uneven or shaped like a dog bone, tadpole, or comma, it means the tip area is dirty or the fluid tip is not firmly seated. Take the gun apart, clean it, and assemble it with all parts seated firmly. The literature for your gun should have an exploded drawing showing the names of all the parts, along with adjustment and assembly information.

To change the pattern from round to oval, turn the air fan control knob counterclockwise. On most guns, this knob is either on the left side of the gun, or it is the uppermost knob on the back edge of the gun. Some HVLP guns can be changed from a round to an oval spray pattern by rotating the air cap 45 degrees. You can change all guns from a vertical oval to a horizontal oval by rotating the air cap 90 degrees. Use the vertical oval pattern when moving the gun left to right, and the horizontal when moving it up and down. In other words, always move the gun at right angles to the fan pattern. For even coating, overlap each pass two-thirds of the way over the previous pass.

Test the fan shape and size first on scrap cardboard. Most guns spray horizontal and vertical ovals and round patterns.

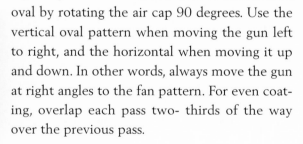

Q How can I avoid drips and runs when I spray?

Avoid drips when you spray by lightening up on the trigger, keeping the gun moving while the trigger is depressed, and making sure you move at right angles to the direction of the fan. Hold the gun parallel to the wood with the tip 8 in. away, and practice before you spray.

The trigger on your gun is like the gas pedal in your car. Air comes out as soon as you pull the trigger, but the farther back you pull it, the more fluid is mixed with the air. You control the flow of finish by how far you pull the trigger. Practice on cardboard to coordinate how fast you must move the gun with how far you pull the trigger. Moving too slowly or pulling the trigger too much will put excess finish on the wood, and may result in sags or runs.

Keep the tip about 8 in. away from the surface, and make sure the gun is always parallel to the wood. Avoid swinging your arm in an arc, or else you'll move the tip too close in the center and too far away at the ends. Pull the trigger only while the gun is moving, starting just before the wood and stopping only after the gun tip passes it. If you stop moving while the trigger is depressed, you'll get runs. Pay attention to the fan direction, and always move the gun at right angles to the long oval shape. Do a dry run. Pay attention to where you move the gun and how much you pull the trigger. Practice spraying the piece of furniture with an empty gun. Think of it as driving the course before a race because knowing what lies ahead gives you an advantage.

Avoid drips by doing a dry run to develop your spray path before you hook up the gun.

Q Is there a trick to spraying the inside corners of my cabinet without getting sags and runs?

Avoid corner drips by adjusting the fan to a small circle and easing up on the trigger. Or, switch to a touchup gun.

Spray the inside corners first. Use a round pattern and a light spray, and get close to the wood.

The wide fan you normally use for larger surfaces will hit the two adjacent sides of an inside corner long before any finish gets into the recess. The key is to reduce the fan pattern, cut back on the trigger, and hit the corners first. Turn the fan adjustment knob fully clockwise to get a round pattern on the gun. Pull the trigger so that only a small amount of finish comes out, and spray the inside corners with the gun only about 4 in. from the wood. If you have a touchup gun, spray the corners with that instead. Return to the oval fan pattern and avoid the corners when you spray the adjacent panels.

Q I usually brush and wipe stain. Is it true that if I spray stain, I'll get better results?

You can spray on stain if you like, but I don't recommend it.

Most stains are more or less self-regulating. If you brush or wipe them on, then wipe them off, they tend to color evenly. However, if you spray them, the uniformity and consistent color of the stain will depend entirely on your spraying ability. If you are a skilled sprayer, go right ahead. On the other hand, you could spray stain on, then wipe it off while it is still wet, using the gun as a faster applicator than a brush or rag.

How do I spray oil-based polyurethane?

*To spray on oil-based polyurethane, thin it with acetone,
mist it onto the wood, then spray on a thin, wet coat.*

You can spray oil-based polyurethane, but if you do it the same way
you spray lacquer, you're sure to get drips and runs. Try this instead:
Thin the polyurethane with acetone to the consistency of skim milk.
Don't spray a wet coat, but instead, spray a light mist onto the wood.
This step is especially important on vertical surfaces. Let the finish
dry for about 10 minutes. The acetone will evaporate, leaving a partially dried mist of polyurethane. Respray the area with another thin,
wet coat. The wet polyurethane will hang onto the partially dried
mist to prevent drips and runs.

Thin polyurethane
with acetone, and
spray a very light
mist coat first. Let it
tack before spraying
a wet coat.

Is there a special trick to spraying a water-based coating?

Spray on a water-based coating as lightly as possible.

The most common problems with a water-based coating come from spraying
it on too heavily. Most clear water-based coatings look milky white in the can
and after you first spray them, but they clear up as they dry. If you
spray the coating on too heavily, it may stay white, dry too slowly, or
sag and run on vertical surfaces.

There's a reason most people spray water-based coatings on too
heavily. When you spray a light coat, it looks pebbly, like the skin of
an orange. The temptation is to spray more until it looks smooth.
But if you leave it alone, in most cases, it will smooth out by the next
day. It's hard to leave a sprayed water-based coating alone if you are
used to spraying lacquer, which never looks better than the minute
you are done spraying. A water-based coating almost always looks
better the next day, so it requires a leap of faith on your part to walk
away from the project once you're done spraying.

Spray water-based lacquer too wet, and it will develop a
white haze and a pebbly orange-peel surface.

How do I deal with the various spraying problems, like blush, overspray, orange peel, bands, and fisheye?

Each problem has a solution. Here's a rundown of the cause and solution for each situation.

- Blush looks like a white cloud caught in the finish, and is usually associated with lacquer. It is caused by moisture trapped in the wet film, and typically occurs in high humidity. Add some retarder (a slower-drying solvent) to the lacquer and respray the area.

- Overspray is finish that dried in the air before it hit the wood. It looks and feels like the surface of sandpaper. Remove it by sanding lightly with 320-grit paper, and spray the next coat a bit wetter.

- Orange peel refers to a rough, pebbly texture like the skin of an orange. It is a mark of poor atomization caused by either insufficient air pressure or a coating that is too thick. Sand it out, then respray with thinner material, or turn up the air pressure on the gun.

- Bands appear as alternate stripes of finish. Every other band looks too dry. It indicates that you did not sufficiently overlap each successive pass with the spray gun. Each swath should overlap the last by two-thirds. Sand lightly with 320-grit paper to remove any roughness, and spray more carefully on your next pass.

- Fisheye, a condition that looks like fish eyes embedded in the lacquer, is caused by pockets of low surface tension. It shows up mostly in water-based and solvent-based lacquers on pieces being refinished. Add fisheye flowout, available from your finish supplier, to all subsequent coats that you spray. You can prevent it by first sealing the wood with a coat of Zinsser SealCoat.

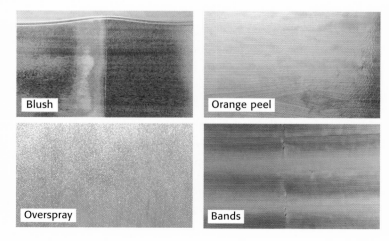

Blush

Orange peel

Overspray

Bands

Q What is French polish? I heard that it is a beautiful but complicated finish.

A The term French polish describes both the material and the method of rubbing shellac onto wood with a cloth pad.

French polish seems to be the Holy Grail of finishing. I've read many conflicting versions of "the only right way to do it," and it seems each gets more complicated than the last.

It's really quite simple. French polishing is a method of rubbing shellac onto wood by hand with a cloth pad. Make a pad by bunching up some cheesecloth inside a square of linen. Twist the loose ends so that the linen forms a smooth, tight surface. Wet the pad with watery-thin shellac and rub it onto the wood. You'll notice that as you squeeze the pad, it feeds more finish onto the surface, so the trick is to squeeze as you rub. If you stop moving, the pad will stick and make a rag mark. Keep moving at all times, even as you touch down and lift off the wood. When the pad gets dry, add more shellac.

Sound tedious? It is. It's quicker to flood the first coat of shellac on and wipe it off. That seals the wood. You can also apply a coat or two with a brush before you switch to the pad. If you have trouble getting the hang of French polishing and the pad sticks or drags when you try to rub, take heart. Zinsser makes a more user-friendly French Polish that prevents sticking pads and makes the process almost foolproof.

Make a French polish pad by wrapping absorbent cotton cloth tightly in a square of linen.

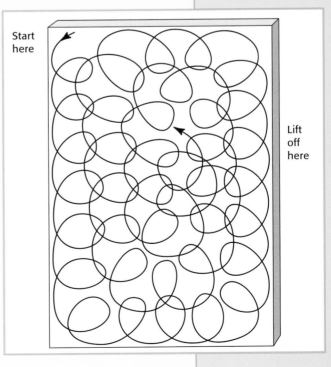

Start here

Lift off here

Keep the pad in motion the entire time, even when you touch down and lift off.

Using Solvents and Strippers

Q. What are the differences between turpentine, mineral spirits, paint thinner, and VM&P naphtha?

For our purposes, these four solvents are mostly interchangeable, but some evaporate faster than others.

All of these solvents are appropriate for thinning and cleaning up waxes, as well as oil-based paints, varnishes, and polyurethanes. Turpentine, the slowest-evaporating solvent, consists of terpines distilled from pine wood. Mineral spirits and paint thinner, two names for exactly the same solvent, evaporate a bit faster. They are mixtures of aliphatic hydrocarbons (which are solvents distilled from petroleum). Odorless mineral spirits are similar, but consist mostly of isoparaffin hydrocarbons that have less of an odor. The fastest-evaporating solvent in this group is Varnish Maker's and Painter's (VM&P) naphtha. It is an aliphatic hydrocarbon mixture, but with a flash point below 100 degrees F. The others have flash points above 100 degrees F.

From left: Paint thinner, odorless mineral spirits, naphtha, and turpentine are all used more or less interchangeably.

Q. I saw a can of MEK at the home improvement store yesterday. What is it and what do I use it for?

MEK, or methyl ethyl ketone, is a flammable solvent used for a variety of coatings.

You've probably seen MEK listed as one of the ingredients in lacquer thinner, but it is also a solvent for oil-based coatings, vinyl sealers, conversion varnish, and for some adhesives. Solvents dissolve specific resins, so use MEK when the label or tech sheet indicates that it is the preferred clean-up solvent or thinner.

Like other lacquer-type solvents, it is quite flammable, so handle it carefully. Since MEK will dry your skin, wear vinyl or latex gloves to protect your hands. It is also considered toxic by inhalation. When you pour MEK or use it, do it in a room with good ventilation and while wearing an organic vapor mask.

MEK is more dangerous than the solvents in the above photo, and warrants the use of gloves, goggles, and a respirator.

Which solvent should I use to thin different finishes, such as lacquer, polyurethane, or shellac?

When in doubt, check the label to determine which solvent is used for thinning finishes or for cleaning up.

Use lacquer thinner for lacquer; denatured alcohol for shellac; and naphtha, mineral spirits, or turpentine for anything oil-based—including polyurethane, paint, and varnish. Avoid thinning water-based coatings if you can, but if you must, you can add up to 10 percent water. For better flow and brushing, you can add Floetrol to water-based paints and coatings, or Penetrol to oil-based materials. Clean up after your project using water-based coatings with a mixture of one cup of household ammonia in a gallon of warm water.

THE RIGHT THINNER	THIN WITH:	CLEAN UP WITH:
Shellac	Denatured alcohol	Denatured alcohol
Lacquer	Lacquer thinner	Lacquer thinner
Oil paint, varnish, or polyurethane	Naphtha, mineral spirits, turpentine, Penetrol	Naphtha, mineral spirits, turpentine
Water-based paint	10% water, Floetrol	Water and ammonia mixture

Is there a limit to how much solvent I can add to a finish?

Be concerned only about how much solvent you add to water-based coatings.

Though it's best to avoid thinning a water-based coating at all, if you must add water, add no more than 10 percent to the mixture.

Feel free to thin most clear coatings as much as you want. Lacquer, shellac, and oil-based polyurethane or varnish will work no matter how much thinner you add. Of course, thinning means less build per coat, since a greater proportion will evaporate. However, it will not change the nature of the coating no matter how thin you make it, so feel free to add thinner until it is easy to work with. Use the appropriate thinner for each coating. Check the chart on this page if you are not sure which to use.

What is retarder? When do I use it, how much should I add, and is there a different one for each finish?

Retarder is a slow-drying solvent for a finish.

Sometimes finishes dry too fast, and that can cause several problems. You may not have enough time to brush smoothly. The finish may dry too fast to allow proper flow and leveling. Moisture can get trapped in spray finishes, which shows up as a white "cloud" called blush. When wiping a finish on and off, you might need more time to coat the entire piece of furniture at once. Whatever the reason, the solution is to add retarder.

Each type of coating has one or more specific types of solvents that work as retarders. Usually the retarders are compatible solvents that evaporate more slowly than what is already in the coating. You'll find some of these solvents in most paint stores, but others are available only through commercial lacquer suppliers or chemical supply companies. In most cases, it is a good idea to add only a small amount to the finish, then retest the coating. Adding too much retarder may result in a finish that won't dry, or stays tacky and soft indefinitely.

Over-the-counter retarders, like Penetrol (for oil-based coatings) and Floetrol (for water-based coatings) have directions on the label indicating how much you can add. Using common solvents requires more judgment and patience. Try your formulas on scrap wood first. Start by adding a small amount, about 10 percent, to the finish, and test for results. In some cases you can go well beyond that. For example, you can safely thin lacquer to about 50/50 with 2-butoxyethanol or other types of commercial lacquer retarders.

Below is a chart of slow and very slow retarders for a variety of common finishes.

RETARDERS	SLOW	VERY SLOW
Shellac	Butyl alcohol	Propylene glycol
Lacquer	2-butoxyethanol, commercial retarders	Propylene glycol, MAK
Oil-based coatings	Turpentine, Penetrol	Boiled linseed oil
Water-based coatings	Floetrol	Propylene glycol

What is acetone and what do I use it for?

Acetone is a very fast-drying, flammable, wide-spectrum solvent used in lacquer, nail polish remover, and for dissolving the adhesive from recalcitrant stickers.

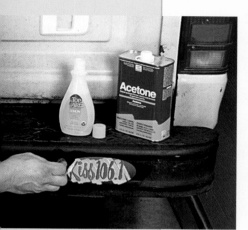

Acetone, found in nail polish remover, is a solvent for nail polish, which is actually lacquer. It will also take off many types of adhesive residue resulting from hard-to-remove labels, masking tapes, and bumper stickers. Use it carefully because it may also remove paint and lacquer, and will soften many plastics.

Acetone can also be used as a reducer for spraying oil-based polyurethane or varnish. Thinning polyurethane with 50 percent acetone allows you to spray a very sparse coat that will get tacky quickly and is less likely to run or sag.

In addition to softening super glue adhesive and removing nail polish, acetone will dislodge stubborn bumper-sticker residue.

Is it true that acetone will dissolve cyanoacrylate (super glue adhesive)?

Yes, it will dissolve super glue adhesive, but it will do so very slowly. You are better off using commercial debonder.

Cyanoacrylate, or super glue adhesive, can be a nightmare when you accidentally glue yourself to something else. Fortunately, most companies that sell the adhesive also sell a debonder to dissolve the bond. Acetone is touted by some as a cheap alternative to commercial debonder, and to be fair, it will work to some degree, especially if you use it before the adhesive has fully cured. However, to separate a cured cyanoacrylate bond using acetone may take up to 24 hours. Clearly, you are much better off with the real deal. The solvent for cyanoacrylate used in a commercial debonder is nitromethane, the same stuff used for "funny car" fuel at race tracks.

Q Do I really need to strip off the old finish if I am going to repaint?

A *If there is any peeling or cracking, strip it, but if the finish is sound, you can paint over it.*

As long as the old finish is still in good shape and holding on to the wood, there is no reason to remove it for repainting. Clean it by scrubbing off any grease or dirt with TSP (trisodium phosphate) or TSP substitute, then sand with 220-grit paper to rough up the surface. Apply a coat of primer before repainting to help the paint bond well to the old finish. On the other hand, if the old finish is cracked or peeling, strip it. If you don't, the new paint will come off with it as the old paint peels.

Q What is the safest, fastest stripper?

A *The safest stripper is the slowest one. Faster strippers require more caution and safety gear.*

I'm afraid you've posed a bit of a conundrum.

The safest stripper, made by 3M and appropriately labeled "Safest Stripper," is also the slowest on the market. Thick finishes may take up to 24 hours to soften, and 3M's stripper is designed to stay wet that long for just that reason. It works well on paint and oil-based finishes, but not as well on lacquer or shellac. On the plus side, it is nonflammable and requires no special ventilation or safety gear.

At the other end of the spectrum are the methylene chloride (DCM)-based strippers. They are fast, nonflammable, and work on any finish. However, they require adequate ventilation, neoprene gloves, goggles, and a respirator. You can also find medium-speed strippers, some of which are flammable, but they too require standard safety gear.

You won't need protective gear for slow Safest Stripper (left), but you'll need to suit up for the harsher fast-acting stuff (right).

Q Are there tricks that make stripping with chemicals easier, or should I just use a heat gun and a scraper?

Bagging and draping make chemical stripping more pleasant and efficient, but heat guns and scrapers have their place too.

You can remove a lot of finish quickly with a scraper, heat gun, or both. They're especially helpful when you have to strip many layers of old paint.

However, you'll find that mechanical stripping won't remove the paint from nail holes, crevices, or large pores in wood. In that case, for taking off thin finishes as well, use paint remover.

The trick to efficient chemical stripping is to keep the paint remover wet until all the finish is completely softened. There are two ways to do that. You can constantly reapply more stripper as it starts to dry, or you can bag or drape the furniture. To bag, apply a thick coat of stripper, then cover the furniture with a large plastic trash bag or clear plastic polyethylene sheeting. The stripper won't dissolve the plastic, but the plastic will substantially retard the rate of evaporation. Lift a corner every so often to see how the stripper is doing.

When the finish is softened enough so that it comes off all the way down to the wood, it is time to remove it. Take off the plastic and use scrapers, scrub brushes, coarse steel wool, or nylon abrasive pads to get the gunk off. Reapply more stripper if you must and keep the wood wet, but make sure all the finish is off before you let the wood dry. If you let the stripper dry while there is still paint in the wood pores or carvings, you may never get it out. Of course, you can always paint it again.

A fuming tent of clear plastic on a frame speeds the process by keeping stripper fumes where they belong.

Is there a way to strip milk paint? None of the strippers I've tried work.

To remove stubborn milk paint, use lye or special milk paint strippers.

You're right. Milk paint is very tenacious, and most normal paint removers will not take it off. The traditional stripper for removing milk paint is lye, but it is very hazardous to handle. You can make a lye stripper by mixing drain-opener crystals with water. Wear gloves and goggles, and always add the lye to the water, not the other way around. A better alternative is to buy special milk paint strippers. Although you won't find them at the home improvement store, at least three companies sell milk paint stripper online (see Resources).

Milk paint resists most strippers, but several companies make special milk paint removers, like the ones shown here.

After I finished stripping an oak chair, I noticed there is still paint in the pores. How do I get it out?

Reapply the stripper, let it sit, then scrub the pores with a stiff bristle brush. If restripping doesn't work, just repaint the chair.

You must keep the wood wet with stripper until all the paint is softened and removed. If you let the piece dry with paint still in pores and crevices, there is a good chance it will be permanent. Since that is what has happened, try reapplying fresh stripper, bag the chair, and give the remover time to soften the paint. When it is soft, scrub diligently with a stiff, natural-bristle brush. Don't use synthetic bristles because they may dissolve in stripper. Afterward, scrub with lacquer thinner and a brush to dislodge any paint remnants. If there is still paint in the pores, decide what color you'd like to paint the chair.

Achieving the Right Color and Sheen

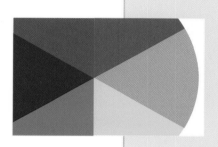

Q How do I prevent stains from blotching?

A *Some stains blotch on some woods. You can prevent blotching by using wood conditioner or by presealing the wood.*

Not all stains blotch, and not all woods are prone to blotching. Some woods will take any stain nicely, and some stains will work with any wood. The first step is to understand when the blotching is likely to occur.

Two different conditions cause blotching. Hidden pockets of sap in certain woods, such as cherry, pine, and most other soft woods, can cause one type of blotching. This type only occurs on these woods, only when you use an oil-based stain that contains dye. Wood with grain that unpredictably changes direction, such as birch, maple, poplar, or any light wood with an erratic grain or figure, will absorb more stain in the areas where the end grain emerges. Since it absorbs more stain, the end grain becomes a darker patch. Uneven staining can occur with both oil- and water-based stains, but usually happens when there is dye in the stain.

Two preventative measures will work in either case. You can apply wood conditioner or preseal the surface. If a manufacturer makes a stain that is likely to blotch, the company will also sell a wood conditioner. Flood it on, wipe it off, then stain while the wood is still wet, since wood conditioner does not work after it dries.

A presealing process is a bit different. Apply a thin coat of SealCoat or wax-free shellac, and then wipe it off while it is still wet. Let it dry before you stain. Both wood conditioner and presealing will limit the amount of stain that remains on the wood and therefore will result in a much lighter stain.

Raw pine and birch may blotch (left). Wood conditioner (middle) and SealCoat (right) prevent blotching but may weaken the stain.

Oak (bottom board) won't blotch under any stain. Pine (top board) will, but pigmented stains (right, on each board) won't cause blotching on any wood.

Q Which woods and which stains are likely to blotch or stain unevenly?

Sappy hardwoods, erratic-grain hardwoods, and most softwoods are prone to blotching or uneven staining. Stains with dye, usually oil-based, are blotch candidates.

A number of woods are likely to stain unevenly and should be considered candidates for wood conditioner or presealing:

- Woods that contain random pockets of sap (such as cherry and almost all softwoods) will blotch, but only when an oil-based stain is used.
- Hardwoods with erratic figure or grain characteristics (such as maple, birch, and poplar), and softwoods that have pronounced bands of early-wood and latewood (such as pine, cedar, spruce, fir, and hemlock) are likely to stain unevenly.

To determine which stains are prone to blotch, check the store shelf for a wood conditioner paired with your brand of stain. If the company that makes your stain also makes a wood conditioner, there is a good chance you will need it. After all, they know best how their stains work.

Some stains (right) don't need wood conditioner, but if the stain company sells it (left), you'll probably need it.

Q How can I prevent end grain from soaking up so much stain?

Prior to staining, sand the end grain with dull garnet paper, or seal it with SealCoat or glue size.

You can sand the end grain with used or dull garnet paper to burnish the wood and somewhat reduce the amount of stain it absorbs. A more effective way to avoid this problem is to first seal the end grain with a coat of SealCoat or glue size. You can make glue size by mixing equal parts of liquid hide glue and water. Brush on a coat of sealer or size and let it dry. Then, sand lightly with 320-grit paper to smooth the surface. Try not to get the mixture on the flat grain of your piece or it will block stain in that spot, too.

Presealing the end grain with SealCoat (left side of panel) will prevent the end grain from absorbing too much stain.

What is the best way to apply stain in order to get a uniform color?

Flood the stain on, then wipe it off while it is still wet.

The best way to apply stain for uniform color is also the easiest way. Flood stain liberally onto the wood, and then wipe it off while it is still wet. Use a brush, rag, nylon abrasive pad, sponge, or spray gun to apply the stain, and then wipe it off with rags or paper shop towels. Some woods absorb more stain than others, but the intensity of the stain will be controlled by how the wood absorbs it, not by how you apply it. To get a deeper color when using commercial stains, let the first coat dry thoroughly, and then repeat the procedure exactly. Don't apply more than two coats of stain before you add a coat of sealer to lock it in.

The best method to achieve uniform color is to flood the stain on liberally, then wipe it off while it's still wet.

Which is better, water-based, oil-based, or dye stains?

Choose a stain by assessing working time, appearance, and compatibility with your topcoat.

Water-based and oil-based commercial stains work equally well, but there are differences in each product that may matter to you. Water-based stains usually dry faster and have a less potent odor. They are compatible under any finish. Oil-based stains dry more slowly, allowing more time to apply and wipe, and in some cases adding more depth and richness to the wood. Most finishes will go over oil-based stains with no problem, but it is best to seal oils with Zinsser SealCoat prior to applying a water-based topcoat.

Dye stains, which are sold as powders, liquid concentrates in solvent, and as ready-to-use liquids, are compatible under water-based or oil-based materials. Some dye stains have a distinctive odor and others do not. Most of them dry very fast and color more deeply than other types of stain.

Q **Which is a better stain, one with pigment or dye?**

Most commercial stains contain both pigment and dye, and each has its own distinctive look.

Figured maple (top) and oak (bottom) were stained with the same color of pigment stain (left side, both boards) and dye stain (right side, both boards).

Pigments and dyes are two common coloring agents used to make stains. Pigments are particles of ground-up colored dirt suspended in a liquid. In addition to the liquid (which evaporates to allow the stain to dry), pigment stains contain a binder. The binder can be any film-forming finish. It acts like glue to bind the pigment to the wood. Pigment particles are fairly large and sit atop wood, finding nooks and crannies in which to lodge. Therefore, pigment stains tend to wipe right off very dense woods, but pack lots of color into woods with large pores.

Dyes are crystals that dissolve in solvent to form molecular-sized particles of colorant. The particles are vastly smaller than pigment particles, so they penetrate deeper into wood and will color even dense woods with no apparent pores. To give you an idea of the difference in size, picture this: If a typical dye particle were the size of a marble, a typical pigment particle would be the size of a '55 Buick.

There are more differences between pigments and dyes:

- Dyes are translucent and can tint wood with vivid, intense color.
- Pigments are opaque, so too much pigment will obscure the wood underneath the color.
- Dye will bring out the subtle figure of a tight-grain wood, like curly maple, but will uniformly color coarse-grained woods.
- Pigment tends to wipe off tight-grain woods, but will enhance the grain pattern of large-pore woods, like oak. Since the stain manufacturer does not know which wood you will stain, most interior stains contain both pigment and dye.
- A dye will most likely fade in sunlight, but a pigment keeps its color in bright sun. Therefore exterior stains contain pigment, but not dye.

Dye (left side) and pigment (bottom) on an oak board. Most commercial stains contain both dye and pigment (bottom left corner of the board).

Q **What is aniline dye and how do I use it?**

Aniline dye is one type of translucent stain. Flood it onto the wood, then wipe it off while it is still wet.

Aniline dye, derived from coal tar, is one of several types of dyes. Since most dyes act alike, and because aniline dyes were the first on the market, many people mistakenly call all dyes "aniline dye." Many dyes sold today are not anilines, so the simpler term "dye" is more accurate.

Dyes add intense color to wood without obscuring its figure or grain patterns. All dyes are translucent, which means that light passes through them. While pigments act like paint, dyes act like stained glass. Although many stains contain dye, you can also buy dyes separately in powdered or liquid form. Dye powders and liquids are formulated to mix with water, alcohol, or petroleum solvents, though some types will mix with all three. Although there are some fairly lightfast dyes, most are fugitive, which means they will fade in sunlight. For that reason, dyes are used only for interior applications.

Dye stains won't penetrate sealed wood, so they are always applied to raw wood. Flood the dye liberally onto the wood, then wipe off as much as you can while it is still wet. That way, the wood will determine how much dye is absorbed. For a more intense color, mix more dye to less solvent. The way to control the dye's intensity is by how you mix it, not by how you apply it to wood. You can also add dye in liquid form to clear finishes to make translucent colored coatings, but make sure the solvent in the dye is compatible with that of the finish.

Pigment (left) is opaque and can obscure the wood grain, but the same color of dye (right) is translucent.

Is it true that water-soluble dyes penetrate wood more deeply than oil-soluble dyes?

Yes, but how deeply depends upon the type of wood.

Woodworkers favor dye-based stains for their ability to penetrate deeply into wood. Pigment stains tend to stay on the surface of the wood. Of the various dyes, water-soluble stains penetrate most deeply; the depth varies with the type of wood. More porous woods allow deeper penetration than denser ones. Water-soluble dye will penetrate to a depth of about 3 to 4 mils in hard maple, 7 to 10 mils in yellow pine, and 12 mils in basswood (1 mil =.001 in.). Oil-soluble dyes, which are actually mixed into solvent, will go into the wood to about half the depth of water-soluble dyes. One advantage of a deeper-penetrating dye is that you are less likely to sand through the color when sanding the finish.

When I try to stain hard maple, the stain seems to wipe right off. How can I get a darker stain?

Use a dye stain instead of a pigment stain.

It's frustrating, but finely sanded hard maple is so dense and smooth that pigment stains tend to wipe right off, leaving very little color behind. There are no pores large enough for the pigment to fill. Combination stains that contain both pigment and dye will color maple a bit better, but the dye portion is doing all the work. The result is that even several applications may not stain maple a dark color. Dyes, however, contain particles small enough to penetrate even dense maple. A dye stain applied to raw maple will darken the wood as much as you like. For a more intense color, increase the ratio of dye to solvent when you mix the stain.

Pigment stains (right) won't penetrate hard maple and leave it barely stained, but the same color of dye (left) deeply stains the maple.

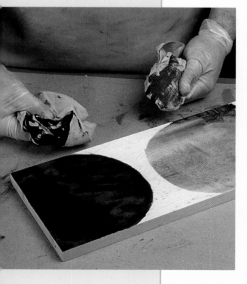

Q Are there tricks for accentuating the grain on curly maple and other figured woods?

A Boiled linseed oil or shellac will pop figured wood grain without adding much color. However, dyes do an even better job of accentuating grain.

Boiled linseed oil pops the grain of figured wood, like this maple, without substantially changing its color.

Figured wood has grain that changes direction so that when it is cut flat, a mixture of end grain and flat grain patterns is exposed. Anything that imparts more color to the end grain than the flat grain, such as a dye, will add contrast to the figure. You can also add depth, or chatoyance, with very little color change. Chatoyance, French for "like a cat's eye," is a term borrowed from the jewelry industry to describe the flip-flop and shimmer of stones like tiger's-eye agate. Figured woods show the same characteristic, and some finishes enhance it.

The best coating to enhance figured wood grain is boiled linseed oil. Use it straight from the can with no solvent added. Flood it onto the wood and let it set for 10 minutes. If it is absorbed completely before that, add more so that the wood stays fully wet the entire time. After 10 minutes, wipe off any oil that was not absorbed. The oil will add a tiny amount of amber color but lots of depth. Wax-free shellac or Zinsser SealCoat will work almost as well to achieve the same effect, and it soaks into the wood in seconds.

For a more dramatic treatment, color the wood with a weak but dark brown or black dye. Flood on the dye and wipe it off immediately. Sand the wood to remove any dye on the surface. The dye will remain in the pores. Then dye the wood with a contrasting light-color dye. The dark and light areas will play off one another to enhance the figure.

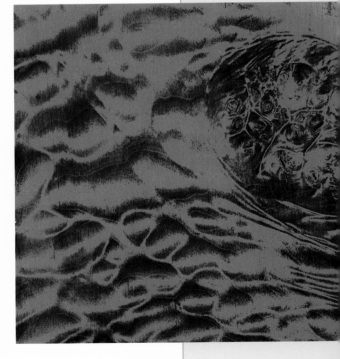

This maple board was dyed with black, sanded, then dyed with red to make the grain pop vividly.

How do I match sapwood to heartwood or get the stain to look uniform on pieces of furniture containing different colors of woods?

Stain the whole piece first, then restain those areas that are lighter or miscolored.

Dyes are better at equalizing the color of different woods and at matching sapwood with heartwood. When you have the option, use a dye stain first, and that may solve the problem in one step. If you can't use dye, don't worry. The following technique works with all types of stain. First, stain the entire piece. After the stain has dried, restain those areas that are too light using either a different color stain, or a second application of the same stain, depending on whether you need to alter the color or merely make it darker. Sometimes, I'll use a small artist's brush or a Q-tip to carefully apply the second stain to the spots where it is needed.

Stain sapwood to match, using a Q-tip as an applicator, or the sapwood streak will stand out, as it does on the side of this box.

On hardwood, black dye (left) looks purple-gray, but India ink (right) makes wood completely black.

How do I ebonize wood?

Use India ink as your stain.

There are a number of ways to use chemicals or stain to ebonize wood. The majority of chemical treatments, like iron buff, make wood dark gray but not very black. Black dye works well on spongy woods, like basswood, but leaves

hardwoods like maple with a blue or purple hue rather than black. To blacken wood, use India ink. India ink is available from art supply stores, and water-based India ink is compatible under virtually every finish. As you do with any stain, flood on the India ink, then wipe off any excess. In rare cases, you may have to stain a second time after the first application dries.

I'm not good at mixing colors. Does anyone sell custom-colored stains?

Yes, your local paint store, because dilute paint works as a pigment stain.

Here's one of the best tricks of the trade. Pigment stains contain the same three basic elements as paint: solvent, binder, and pigment. Mix any paint 50/50 with the appropriate solvent, and you have an excellent pigmented or "wiping" stain. Choose your custom color from the wall of paint chips, take it to the counter, and have them mix you a quart. Take it home and thin it to produce twice as much stain. Use water for thinning latex and mineral spirits for oil-based paints.

Mix any custom-tinted paint 50/50 with its solvent and —voilà!—you have a custom, pigmented wood stain. Here, latex paint is being thinned with water.

Can you give me any advice on how to mix custom stains and glazes?

Use artist's oils and Japan colors for for making oil-based stains, artist's acrylics for water-based stains, or Universal Tinting Colors (UTCs) for either.

A stain or glaze is a mixture of pigment, binder, and solvent. Varying the ratios will change the drying time and intensity of color. Mix oil-based stains and glazes with artist's oils, or for faster-drying stains, mix with Japan colors. Thin the color pastes with mineral spirits, and add a small amount of boiled linseed oil for body. More linseed oil will give you more time to manipulate the stain or glaze before it dries. To make a water-based stain, thin artist's acrylic colors with water and add a small amount of clear water-based finish as a binder. Extend the drying time by adding propylene glycol, available at some pharmacies, all chemical supply houses, and most cigar stores. (A 50/50 mixture of propylene glycol and water is used as the charging solution for the humidifiers in cigar humidors.) UTCs, which are available at some woodworking specialty stores, will work with both mediums.

Q **I never seem to know which color to add when I'm mixing custom stains. Is there a simple way to learn this?**

Consult a color wheel, or, easier still, memorize the three basic color pairs: red/green, yellow/purple, orange/blue.

Take a look at the color wheel on this page. The colors directly opposite one another are called complementary colors. As you can see, they are the Christmas colors (red and green), the Easter colors (purple and yellow) and the Denver Bronco's colors (blue and orange). You may not always have a color wheel nearby, but it is easy enough to remember these three pairs. Whenever you add two complementary colors together, they neutralize one another. If a stain is too red, add a bit of green, and it will disable the red. This is true of wood color as well; wood that is too greenish can be corrected with a reddish stain.

It's often difficult to figure out which complementary color to add to a stain that appears to be brown. The stain may be too reddish-brown or too greenish-brown, and it requires concentration to figure out which color to add to neutralize the hue. You'll find that with a little practice, it will come easily. Try mixing some stains and practicing on scrap wood to get the hang of how to mix a custom stain.

When you attempt the real thing, keep records for your reference. Measure and record the amounts of each material you add. Make small batches first to test on wood scraps, and when the color is right, make up a larger batch. By writing down your formulas, you can scale up to reproduce as much of the color as you need, either now or months later when you decide to make a matching piece.

Color Wheel

The complementary colors, which neutralize one another, are directly opposite each other on the color wheel.

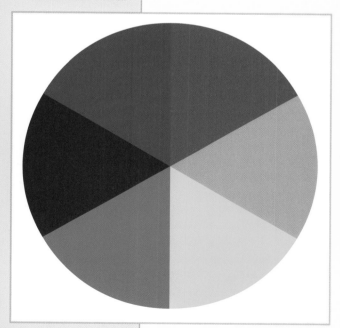

Q What is a chemical stain and what is it used for?

Chemical stains are chemicals that react with wood to create color and are used mostly for specialty staining.

Before aniline dyes were first produced in 1856, very few natural dyes worked with wood. Instead, finishers found chemicals that changed color when they reacted with wood. These chemical stains, which are often toxic, hazardous, and unpredictable, were largely abandoned once synthetic dyes became available. However, there are a few jobs that chemical stains do best. For example, potassium dichromate will color mahogany a dark red but won't affect tannin-free woods, such as holly. Even today, finishers use it to keep holly inlays and stringers white while staining the surrounding mahogany cordovan red.

Potassium dichromate, a chemical stain, colors this mahogany board (above) dark brown but leaves the holly inlay almost untouched.

Q What is fumed oak and how is it done?

Fuming is the chemical stain process of exposing wood to strong ammonia fumes.

We can credit Gustav Stickley with our current awareness of fumed oak, because he quite often used the process on his furniture. If you expose a wood that contains tannin to strong ammonia fumes, it will turn dark. White oak, used by Stickley, contains lots of tannin, and turns a very dark brownish gray when fumed. The exact color depends on the length of time it is exposed and the temperature of the air in the chamber.

Use a strong 28 percent concentration of ammonia, such as the type in blueprint machines. Place it in open bowls with the raw, sanded furniture and seal both in a plastic tent for one to four days. Be very careful handling the ammonia, as it is both extremely irritating and toxic. Wear goggles, gloves, and a good respirator, and limit your exposure as much as possible.

Leave an oak piece in a chamber with strong (28 percent solution) ammonia fumes and it will turn dark brownish gray.

Q Can I stain mahogany to a lighter color?

A No, not exactly, but you can make it brighter with yellow dye, or bleach it to make it lighter.

It's easy to darken wood with a stain, because stains add color, but to make wood lighter you must remove color. A yellow dye stain will brighten up some woods like mahogany and walnut by adding highlights, but it won't remove any color. The only way to remove color is to bleach the wood. Two different materials are sold as wood bleach. One, oxalic acid, will only remove stains from wood but will not bleach it. True wood bleach is sold as a two-bottle set containing strong concentrations of lye and peroxide. Apply the peroxide to the raw wood, then apply the lye before the peroxide evaporates. The reaction of the two chemicals will bleach the wood. Let the wood dry overnight, and then wash it with plenty of clean water to neutralize any bleach residue. Both chemicals are caustic and require gloves, goggles, and a respirator during handling.

Two-part wood bleach removes the color from these maple, walnut, and mahogany boards.

Q Is there any way to speed up the natural graying process of raw wood?

A No, but you can mimic this aged look with pigment stains.

It's unusual to hear of someone who wants things to age faster. Most of my friends are trying to slow down the aging process.

The sample at left is a good example of what you can do with common finishing materials. I scrubbed this cedar board with a wire brush to create the texture of aged wood, then stained it with driftwood-colored pigment stain to mimic the look of grayed wood. If you do a good job and have it viewed from a distance, you may fool all but the most astute observers.

You can make convincing weathered-looking gray wood by wire-brushing the wood, then applying driftwood color stain.

Q **Is there a way to get a Mission oak color without fuming?**

Yes, and it's quite easy. Use either asphaltum or Minwax Jacobean stain.

The dark, brown oak color known as Mission style is fairly easy to obtain using asphaltum-based stains, and is better than the color produced by fuming. You can make a traditional asphaltum stain by reducing four parts Sherwin Williams' Gilsonite concentrate with four parts mineral spirits and one part boiled linseed oil. Easier still, use Minwax Jacobean stain straight from the can without reducing it. With either stain, flood it on and wipe it off. Let it dry overnight, and if it is still not dark enough to suit you, do a second application. Once it is dry, topcoat the piece with shellac, lacquer, or oil-based polyurethane.

Minwax Jacobean and Sherwin Williams' Gilsonite both make convincing Mission Oak stains so you don't have to resort to fuming methods.

Q **How can I achieve the dark shellac finish I see on antique furniture?**

Apply a coat of garnet shellac, or use SealCoat modified with alcohol-soluble dye.

You can get the aged look of antique furniture by buying and mixing colored shellac flakes, or by adding dye to shellac in liquid form. Shellac flakes are sold in various colors as well as in different degrees of refinement. Dark garnet flakes are close to the color of aged shellac. Mix 4 oz. ounces of dewaxed garnet flakes into a pint of denatured alcohol and apply as many coats as you deem necessary. If you don't fancy mixing flakes, buy some Zinsser SealCoat, which is dewaxed shellac, and add some alcohol-soluble dye. Liquid dye concentrates can be added straight into the shellac, but if you use dye powders, dissolve them in alcohol first. SealCoat is sold in paint stores, but shellac flakes and dyes are not. (You can buy them at www.homesteadfinishing.com.)

To mimic the color of aged shellac, use garnet shellac flakes (top, right) or add dye to either SealCoat or blond shellac (bottom right).

Q How can I reproduce the very uniform dark-cherry finishes I see in furniture stores?

A Tinted lacquer, sprayed onto the wood after it is sealed, will create a uniform dark-cherry finish. Stain the piece, seal it, and then spray tinted lacquer to produce even coloration.

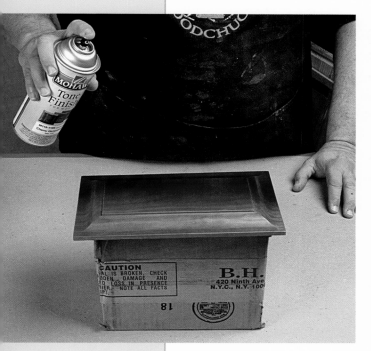

Aerosol cans of tinted lacquer (available from Mohawk and Behlen) let you copy the look of commercial furniture that has been sprayed with toner.

This technique is a great way to make plain or even mismatched woods look uniform. Tinted finish hides so much of the original color and grain pattern of the wood that it will make alder, poplar, maple, fruitwood, and cherry all look the same. Here's how to do it.

Stain the raw wood with a dark-cherry stain lighter than the desired final color. The stain will help blend the various wood tones and limit the color variation from board to board. Seal it with a coat of Zinsser SealCoat. Additionally, stain and seal several scrap boards of the same wood. Choose the topcoat you plan to spray, and tint it using predissolved dyes. Most likely, the tinting will be a dark reddish-brown color. Mix a small amount, keeping track of your formula, and test it on the sample boards. When the color is right, mix a larger batch.

Spray cautiously and lightly because it is easy to go overboard. Use a small touchup gun if you have it, or adjust your gun to spray a small, controllable fan width. Work in good lighting and tint the piece until it is as dark as you'd like and uniform in color. Let the tint coat dry, then add two or three more coats of clear finish in whatever sheen you have chosen. Commercial finishes are typically satin or semigloss sheen.

Old mahogany furniture sometimes has a rich brown finish with golden highlights. How can I create that color on new mahogany?

You can create that rich brown finish on mahogany furniture, but it's a multistep finish with at least four color coats. Add highlights with a yellow or orange dye, seal, fill the pores with a contrasting color, then stain, seal, and glaze.

What you describe is a wonderful finish with a deep red-brown color offset by lighter background tones, and it works for both mahogany and walnut.

First, add highlights after sanding by staining the raw wood with a yellow or orange water-soluble dye. Flood it on and wipe it off immediately, leaving just enough to turn mahogany's characteristic pinkish cast golden. Seal the wood with a thin coat of Zinsser SealCoat.

Mix a pore filler in a cordovan red color to contrast with the wood. Fill the pores, remove the excess filler, and let it dry. Sand it lightly with 320-grit paper to remove any residue, but don't sand through the sealer. If you do sand through and remove any of the dye, touch up the spots with more dye before you continue. At this point you should have wood with dark red-brown pores against a golden-orange background. Now it's time to blend the colors together.

Stain the wood with a reddish-brown pigment stain, flooding it on and wiping it off evenly so that it colors but does not obscure the wood. Let the stain dry, and then seal it with a coat of lacquer or oil-based polyurethane, whichever you will use for your topcoat. Stain over the finish (called glazing) with thinned asphaltum or Minwax Jacobean stain, to blend the colors and add depth. When the glaze is dry, add several coats of lacquer or polyurethane, sanding between coats to level the pores.

This "step sample" was dyed, pore-filled, stained, and finally glazed to create the deep, rich, brown mahogany color at the bottom.

How do I stain both birch and mahogany so that they look the same?

You can stain birch the color of mahogany, but because the grain pattern is different, it will merely look like stained birch.

Birch absorbs stain well, and if you apply a mahogany-colored stain to it, you'll have mahogany-colored wood. However, birch is a closed-grain wood and mahogany is an open-grained wood. That means mahogany has large, visible pores and birch does not. You can't match the texture, but with the right color stain, you can make mahogany and birch look similar enough to appear convincing to onlookers from across the room. If you need to stain a piece of furniture that is part mahogany and part birch or another light-colored wood, stain twice. First, stain the entire piece the color you want for the mahogany. Once the stain is dry, restain just the birch parts with a different color, mixed so that it matches the stained mahogany.

It takes at least two staining steps to make birch (top board) look similar to stained mahogany (bottom board).

I'd like to match a piece of furniture I made with our store-bought dining set. Is there some way to do that?

Yes, but it is not easy. You must re-create the coloring sequence of the original piece of furniture.

Most commercial furniture is colored in several steps, which may include dye stains on the raw wood, pigment stains, glazes (stains floated between coats of finish), and toners (tinted topcoats). In order to match such a complicated coloring sequence, you must re-create it. That means cracking the code of how it was done and reproducing it. Look into the finish under good light and try to identify the layers of color. Experience with many coloring techniques will teach you what each looks like and how it changes wood, and will prepare you for this sort of finishing detective work.

Q What are the steps for creating a distressed finish?

A There are several ways to achieve a distressed finish. Color distressing means that you add swooshes and flyspecks. Physical distressing means re-creating a damaged, worn look, either before or after the finish is applied.

There are several different distressed looks. The simplest way to distress a surface is done solely with color, by adding tiny dark dots called "flyspecks" and thin dark swooshes that are supposed to look like dirty scratches. After the wood is colored and sealed, make random scratch marks with a dark touchup marker. To create flyspecks, dip an old toothbrush or stencil brush into thick dark-colored stain, hold it near the wood, and flick the bristles with your finger to spray the wood with tiny dots of color. If you mess up, simply wipe it off before it dries and try again; that's why you flyspeck on sealed wood. After the flyspecks are dry, add another coat of two of topcoat to seal them and smooth the surface.

Physical distressing, which mimics worn furniture, is more fun to achieve. You get to beat up the furniture, either before or after you finish it. Sand the surface as you would normally, then use keys, chain, pliers, files, or anything metal that will add a variety of nicks, dents, and scratches. Make it convincing by concentrating on areas that normally get more wear, like the feet and arms of chairs and the edges of tables. Afterward, sand lightly with 180-grit paper to remove any lifted wood fibers, and when you apply the stain, it will accentuate the damages.

The other option is to add dings and dents after applying the finish. In addition to making nicks and dents, you can use coarse steel wool or sandpaper to wear through the edges and corners of painted furniture.

The handmade "distressing tool" sitting on this new step stool helped create the finish that makes this piece of furniture look old and worn.

To make this tool, embed screws, nails, and screw eyes in a rounded block to produce a variety of distress marks in new wood.

Which finish will give me a natural, woody look?

Any finish can look natural and woody if it is applied thinly enough.

Any finish—polyurethane, Danish oil, boiled linseed oil—applied thin and wiped off will leave the wood looking natural.

The secret to a natural, woody look is not in the finish you use, but in how much you apply to the surface. Any finish will look natural and woody if it is applied in thin coats. Thin finishes don't hide the texture of the wood, and that's what makes them look natural. Of course, there is a trade-off. Thin finishes provide less protection than the same material applied in thicker coats.

Virtually any finish that wipes on and off will result in a natural look, including boiled linseed oil, tung oil, Danish oil, teak oil, shellac, varnish, and polyurethane. Even lacquer will look woody if you omit the sanding sealer and spray only one or two coats onto the wood. Whatever finish you choose, keep it thin, and spray or wipe instead of brushing.

I like thick, satin finishes, but they never turn out as clear as I'd like. What am I doing wrong?

Build the bulk of the finish with gloss coating, making only the last coat or two satin.

For a deep, clear, satin finish, build up coats of gloss. Switch to satin for only the last two coats.

Satin and semigloss coatings contain "flatting agents," which are solid particles floating in the finish. They reduce gloss by diffracting light, while gloss surfaces reflect light. Unfortunately, flatting agents also reduce the clarity of the coating. It makes very little difference on a thin finish, because there is not enough to matter, but thick satin finishes often look cloudy. The solution is to build the bulk of the finish using a clear gloss version of the coating and to use satin only for the last one or two coats. That will give you a thick coating with good clarity and the right sheen.

Q How many coats of (varnish, shellac, lacquer, polyurethane, etc.) finish do I need to apply?

A *Brushing builds up a finish more quickly than spraying or wiping. Some finishes build up more slowly because they have low solids content.*

There are no hard and fast rules about how many coats of any finish you must apply. But that's not to say there are no limits. Lacquer will crack if applied too thickly, and too thin a coating will offer little protection to the wood. Naturally, we expect less protection from intentionally thin coatings, like Danish oil. As a rule, a thin finish provides less protection, but a more natural, woody look. You must make the choice based on what you want the finish to look like versus how durable it must be. For most coatings, a good rule of thumb is to apply at least three or four coats.

The method of application also affects the build of the finish. Brushing deposits more finish per coat than either spraying or wiping, and not surprisingly, some folks apply finish with a heavier hand. Typically, one brushed coat will equal about two sprayed coats or at least four wiped-on coats.

Finally, consider the content of solids in a coating. Solids are the remaining materials left on the wood after the solvent evaporates. Some Danish oil mixtures and lacquers have as little as 10 percent solids, meaning nine-tenths of what you apply evaporates. In contrast, many water-based polyurethanes are 30 percent solids or higher, so one coat will deposit three times as much finish. At the top end is pure boiled linseed oil, which is 100 percent solids. To ascertain how many coats you need, consider your application method, how heavy a hand you have, the solids content of your finish, how much durability you need, and the look you want.

HOW MANY COATS TO APPLY

	MINIMUM # COATS	MAXIMUM # COATS
Shellac or lacquer	2 brushed / 4 sprayed	5 brushed / 10 sprayed
Oil or Danish oil	3 wiped	20 wiped
Varnish or polyurethane	2 brushed / 4 sprayed	6 brushed / 12 sprayed
Water-based coatings	2 brushed / 4 sprayed	4 brushed / 8 sprayed

Q **Try as I might, I can never get satin or gloss finishes to come out perfectly smooth and free of dust nibs. What's the secret?**

A *The secret to a perfect, smooth finish is to rub it out after it is cured.*

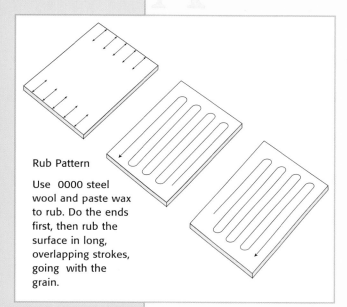

Rub Pattern

Use 0000 steel wool and paste wax to rub. Do the ends first, then rub the surface in long, overlapping strokes, going with the grain.

For smooth satin finishes, apply ample pressure while rubbing the entire surface from side to side in straight lines. Repeat this process at least six times.

It's almost impossible to apply a perfectly smooth coating, but rubbing out the finish will eliminate brush marks, spray texture, and dust nibs. The longer the finish has cured, the easier it is to rub. Wait a minimum of two or three days before rubbing out satin finishes and at least a month to rub out gloss.

For a satin sheen, start by sanding the cured surface with 400-grit self-lubricating sandpaper. Sand just enough to remove any dust nibs, brush marks, or spray texture, and leave the surface perfectly flat and smooth. Dip a pad of 0000 steel wool into paste wax and use it to rub the surface in long straight strokes going with the grain, adding more wax as needed for lubrication. Overlap each stroke and repeat the process several times to ensure that all areas develop a fine, uniform scratch pattern. Wipe off the wax with a clean, dry cloth or shop towel. Mist cold water onto the surface and rub with the grain once more, this time very lightly, using a new 0000 steel wool pad to remove any wax buildup.

To rub to a gloss sheen, sand the finish in succession with 600-, 800-, and 1200-grit papers until it is glass-smooth. Using a damp cloth or a power buffer equipped with a lamb's-wool or foam polishing head, buff the surface with rubbing compound to remove any sanding scratches. Wipe off any residue and repeat the process using polishing compound, which is a finer abrasive than rubbing compound. Wipe off any water and polishing compound residue and inspect your work.

Which finishes can I rub to a satin or gloss finish? Are there any that can't be rubbed?

Any finish can be rubbed if it is thick enough and fully cured.

In theory, all finishes can be rubbed, provided they are thick enough and cured enough. Rubbing starts with sanding, which removes small amounts of finish. The finish must be thick enough so that you don't wear through to raw wood. Most film-forming finishes require a minimum of three brushed coats or six sprayed coats. Because gloss finishes entail more sanding, it is a good idea to apply them even thicker. It is equally important for the finish to be cured. A power buffer creates friction and heat and may actually peel uncured finish off the wood. Wait at least a month before buffing a gloss finish.

In practice, the more brittle a finish is, the easier it is to rub. Brittle finishes, such as shellac and lacquer, rub more easily than soft ones, such as spar varnish. Most wipe-on finishes are applied too thin to rub, but since they get wiped off as well, they usually come out smooth during application. If you like, you can wax a wipe-on finish gently using 0000 steel wool as the applicator to give the surface an especially smooth feel.

Can I use auto body compound to rub out gloss finishes?

Yes. In fact, that's what I use.

Auto body rubbing and polishing compounds are convenient, inexpensive, and easy to use. They are my first choice for rubbing out gloss finishes. While you are at the auto parts store, you might also want to pick up swirl-mark remover or glaze. These liquids are designed to be wiped onto and off a polished surface to add an extra measure of shine.

Common rubbing, polishing, and glazing compounds from the auto body store are perfect for gloss furniture, too.

Repairing Finishing Disasters

While I was sanding a maple and walnut desk, dark sanding dust lodged in the maple's pores. How can I get the dust out?

You can usually scrub dark dust out of raw wood with a stiff bristle brush or sand the wood with a finer grit.

As long as the wood is still unfinished, you can usually scrub dust out of the pores with a dry, stiff bristle brush. As you scrub, lift the dust from the wood with the hose from your shop vac. That way, you won't reintroduce any dust onto the piece. You will find that sanding mixed woods with a finer-grit papers, such as 220 or 320, will also solve the problem. There are fewer scratches into which dust can lodge on finely sanded wood surfaces.

Use a clean scrub brush, or sand to a finer grit, to remove dark sanding swarf from light wood.

I just put a coat of clear Danish oil finish on cherry wood and it turned blotchy. How do I fix this?

Sometimes, adding more of the same finish to the surface will clear up the blotches. If blotches remain, you might have to resort to adding a light stain to the wood.

Many natural or clear Danish oil mixtures contain small amounts of stain. Unfortunately, that can make certain woods, such as cherry, appear uneven or blotchy. Even boiled linseed oil is amber enough to cause problems. The uneven look may diminish as more coats are added. Try adding another coat or two to see if the blotchy look goes away. If not, try adding a light, cherry-colored stain over the oil after it dries. If you choose a stain color close to the color of the wood itself, it will make the entire piece more uniform without excessively altering the color.

How do I get a motor oil stain out of the raw wood top of a dresser I am building?

First use a lacquer thinner wash to sop up as much of the motor oil as you can, then, follow with an ammonia scrub. Finally, hide the remains of the spot with an application of finishing oil.

A drippy can of motor oil can stain raw wood. Scrub it with lacquer thinner to remove most of it.

The good news is that motor oil is a nondrying oil, so it will stay wet for an indefinite time, making it easier to remove. The strategy is to draw the bulk of the oil out of the wood by thinning it, then removing what you can from the surface. After that, an ammonia wash will remove even more oil from the surface, and you can hide whatever oil stain remains with a coat of drying oil used as your first finish coat.

The steps are easy. First, flood the stained wood with lacquer thinner, which is a solvent for the oil. Sop up the thinner-and-motor-oil mixture with paper shop towels. Do this several times to get as much oil out of the wood as possible. Wipe off the wood and let it dry before you move on to step two, an ammonia wash.

Scrub the wood with a nylon abrasive pad dipped in a of a cup of household ammonia in a quart of warm water. Flood the spot, and as before, sop up the liquid with shop towels. Let the wood dry overnight. Most, if not all, of the stain should be removed. If a shadow remains, you can hide it by choosing a wash of drying oil as your first coat of finish. A coat of linseed oil or tung oil, flooded on and wiped off after 10 minutes, will add depth and a slight amber cast to the wood. It should hide the remnants of the motor oil stain, as well.

Coating the entire surface with tung oil or boiled linseed oil will almost completely hide the motor oil stain.

Q **T**he stain I applied appeared to be the right color in the can, but it came out too dark on the wood. Is there any way to fix the color?

A *If there is no other finish on the surface, you can usually scrub off most of the dark stain with lacquer thinner and a nylon abrasive pad.*

Most dye stains are easily reversed using a wash of household laundry bleach, but commercial stains contain pigment and binders as well, and bleach won't affect them. If the stain is fresh, and you have not sealed it with a topcoat, you can scrub some of the stain off.

To do this, use a fairly coarse nylon abrasive pad and lacquer thinner. Soak the stained wood first, and let the lacquer thinner sit and soften the stain for a minute, then add more as you scrub with the pad. As you loosen the stain, mop up as much as you can with paper shop towels, working an area at a time. Repeat the process until no more stain is visible in the scrub liquid. If you have already sealed the stain, you'll have to strip off the finish first.

Once the bulk of the pigment is gone, dry the wood and remove any dye with full- strength household laundry bleach. Apply it evenly with a nylon pad or a synthetic bristle brush (bleach eats natural bristles), and let it dry overnight. Wash the surface with clean water the next day, let the wood dry, and restain with the right color.

Don't give in to the temptation to sand the stain entirely off. Sanding stain will create spotty patches. It takes a large amount of elbow grease and sandpaper to sand all the stain off, and you will have sanded away much of the wood or you may sand right through the veneer.

You can scrub some of a dark stain (top) off with naphtha or lacquer thinner, but only if it is not sealed.

The stain came out uneven—darker in some areas than others. Can I make it uniform without removing what's already on the wood?

Restain only the light areas with the same color stain, or mix a new color in order to make the light areas match.

You can make an uneven stain job more uniform as long as you don't mind matching the darker color. A second application of the same stain, limited to the light areas, will usually produce a uniform color. In extreme cases you might have to mix a darker custom stain. The first coat of stain seals the wood as it dries. As a result, the second coat of stain will not "grab" as aggressively, so it will be easier to control the color by wiping off more or less. Use a clean, dry, soft bristle brush to blend the stain smoothly from one area to the next.

Restaining lighter areas with the same stain will often make them blend nicely with the darker areas.

Staining with complementary colors, like blending red and green here, will change the tint dramatically, especially when using dyes.

Can I change the color of the stain after it is on the wood?

You can alter a color—sometimes dramatically—by restaining with a different hue.

A second application of stain can make the wood darker, but the right stain can also shift the color entirely. For example, if a stain is too red, you can mitigate it by restaining the surface with a greenish stain. Green is red's complementary color, and the two colors cancel out one another, leaving the wood a more neutral brown. Purple and yellow, another complementary pair, also neutralize one another, as do blue and orange. This technique works particularly well with dye stains, but it will work with pigment stains too, even if the surface has a coat of clear finish on it. One word of warning: Applying a light-colored pigmented stain over a darker stain can make the wood appear muddy. Test stain combinations on scrap wood first.

Q My sander fell and dented the wood I was sanding. How do I fix a dent too deep to sand out?

A *Steam will remove dents in raw wood, but only dents, and not gouges.*

Steam will take dents out of raw wood, but gouges are another matter. Dents are depressions in wood where the wood fibers are crushed, but not cut. Gouges are areas where the wood fibers are cut or sections of wood are removed. If you are not sure which you have, try steaming first. If that doesn't work, you can always fill the void with putty.

Wood fibers are like a bundle of hollow straws. When wood is dented, the straws collapse and compress. Steaming restores the fibers to their original shape, eliminating the dent.

To steam a dent, first heat up a clothes iron or soldering iron—anything that will bring lots of heat to a surface quickly. Add a few drops of water to the dent and let it soak in for a few seconds. When it is absorbed, add another drop or two to fill the void. Cover the area with a damp cloth and quickly press the hot iron onto the cloth over the spot. The damp cloth will prevent the iron from scorching the wood, and the hot iron will quickly turn the water into steam. The pressure from the expanding steam removes the dent by uncrushing the wood fibers.

Most dents will come out in one steaming, but severe dents may require a second or third application of water and heat. Repeated steaming may leave a watermark in the wood that can show up during staining. To avoid a watermark, wet the entire surface while you are adding drops of water to the dent. Let the wood dry completely, then sand lightly with 320-grit paper to remove the whiskers of raised grain before staining.

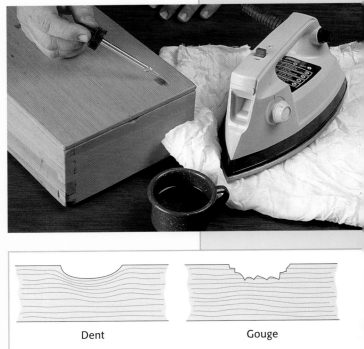

Put a drop of water in the dent, cover it with a damp cloth, and steam it out with an iron.

Dent   **Gouge**

A dent has only crushed fibers; a gouge has wood missing and can't be steamed.

How can I avoid runs when I brush or spray finish?

Use a damp but unloaded brush to smooth out runs while they are still wet. Cut or scrape off hardened drips.

It is easy to smooth out runs and drips if you can catch them while they are wet. To do this, first unload your brush by scraping the bristles across the edge of your paint tray. Use the still-damp bristles to smooth the runs or brush out sags. When you are spraying slow-drying finishes, such as oil-based polyurethane,, keep a brush dampened with mineral spirits handy to quickly fix runs. Fast-drying finishes, like lacquer and water-based coatings, set up too quickly for this technique. Do not try to brush a partially cured spray lacquer or water-based coating or else you'll end up with a choppy-looking mess.

For drips that you don't see until the finish is partially cured, let the run dry completely. Drying may take several days for a thick blob of oil-based varnish. Check the bulb, or round part of the drip, by pressing your thumbnail into it to ensure that it is solid. Use a single-edge razor blade or a very sharp chisel held at a shallow angle to cut off the drip and make it flush with the surrounding finish.

Brittle, fast-drying finishes, such as shellac and lacquer, shrink during drying, causing the runs to diminish considerably during the curing time. These coatings are too brittle to cut. Instead, use the razor blade like a tiny scraper. Hold the blade at 90 degrees to the surface and scrape off the hardened run. After you've cut or scraped the drips, sand the surface lightly with 320-grit paper, then add another thin coat of finish to blend and hide your repair work.

To remove a run, first test the bulb of the drip with your thumbnail to ensure that it is not still liquid inside.

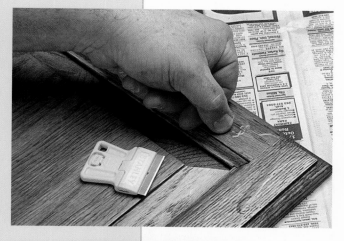

When the drip is dry, slice it off with a sharp razor blade.

Q **How can I fix polyurethane that is still tacky two
days after I brushed it on my project?**

A *Place the finished piece in a warm room with low humidity and wait, or strip it off and start over.*

First, put the tacky piece of wood in a warm,
dry room and give it more time to harden. Oil-
based varnishes, stains, and polyurethanes dry
by reacting with the oxygen in the air. Most
chemical reactions, including this one, accelerate as the temperature rises. As a result, finishes
dry faster in a warm room than in a cold one.

The oil-modified resins used in stains and finishes dry slowly. To overcome this, formulators
add "driers" that act as a catalyst to speed up drying. For example, one coat of raw linseed oil may
take seven days to dry, but the same coat with
driers added will cure in one day. Unfortunately,
very high humidity can disable the driers and
turn a moderately fast-drying finish into a very
slow one. It's best to dry in a room with 50 percent relative humidity or lower.

Certain driers can also be rendered ineffec-
tive over time, particularly in flat, satin, or pigmented formulations. Though this is not a problem for all brands or gloss formulations, driers
will be most effective when you use fresh materials. Older cans of finish may develop drying
problems.

Whatever the cause, your best bet is to create ideal drying conditions and give the finish
more time, even if that means waiting a week or
longer. Given enough time, the finish will even-
tually cure. However, if you are impatient, you can always strip the finish off
and start over with a fresh can and a more effective drying environment.

When the room is
very cold and wet,
finish cures much
more slowly. Crank
up the heat and
wait it out.

Will wood warp if I stain only one side, then stain the other side hours later?

No, it's not likely, and more important, it won't matter.

It's highly unlikely that any stain will cause wood to warp merely because you applied it on one side some time before the other. Most stains are oil- or solvent-based and will not warp wood. Water-based stains are not likely to cause wood movement either, because they dry so quickly. But even if a board did warp after you put water on it, allow it to dry and it will return to its original shape by itself.

Some scratches showed up on the surface when I stained the wood. Can I hide them?

Sometimes, but not always. Sand out the scratches and restain the area. Or add a second stain if you prefer a darker color.

When scratches show up during staining, you can usually stop, wipe off stain, resand the area to remove the scratches, and then restain. It's important to use the same grit and type of paper that you used for the final sanding before stain was applied. Sanding with a finer or coarser grit will cause the stain in the sanded spot to appear darker or lighter than the surrounding area. As long as the stain is still wet, or at least recently applied, this technique usually results in a fairly invisible repair. If the stain is fully cured, or if you've already applied sealer, use more stain without sanding. Applying a glaze— which is another coat of stain on top of the sealer—will make the piece darker, but will help hide the scratches. Let the glaze dry before adding clear finish.

If sanding scratches show up during staining, stop and wipe off all the stain by using its solvent.

Immediately sand out the scratches with the last grit paper you used, then restain.

Q **After I applied Danish oil to oak, the finish turned rough and pebbly the next day. What went wrong?**

A *Danish oil can bleed out of large pores and harden into nubs. You have three choices: Keep wiping the surface; sand and reapply; or switch finishes.*

On oak, Danish oil tends to "walk" out of pores and dry to hard nubs at the mouth of the wood's large pores.

What you describe is common for how Danish oil finishes react on some woods. The finish permeates the large pores of woods like oak, ash, and mahogany, and after you wipe off the excess, it continues to bleed out of the pores. Leave it alone and it will collect at the mouth of each pore and dry into tiny hard beads of finish, making the formerly smooth surface as rough as sandpaper. To avoid this, you can rewipe the surface every hour or so until the bleeding stops, or wait and sand off the hard nubs the next day. Both options are tedious. I prefer not to use Danish oil on large-pore woods. An unthinned coat of oil varnish or boiled linseed oil wiped on and off will give you the same look without the bleeding problems.

Q **I've tried spray guns, paint pads, and brushes, but I still get tiny air bubbles in water-based finishes. What am I doing wrong?**

If all else fails, you can diminish foaming by adding an ounce of half-and-half to your water-based coating.

A *Before application, stir in 1 oz. of half-and-half per quart of clear finish to help prevent foaming.*

Foaming, or tiny air bubbles trapped in the finish, is a common problem with water-based coatings. Sometimes bubbles show up even if your application tools and techniques are perfect. Don't despair. Just before you brush or spray, stir an ounce of half-and-half (coffee creamer) into the finish. The butterfat in half-and-half acts as a defoamer to help eliminate the air bubbles. Because the creamer is homogenized, it mixes easily into water-based finishes, just as it does into coffee.

Q How do I fix the several glue spots that appeared at the joints after I stained the wood?

If the wood is not sealed, you can get rid of glue spots by scraping, sanding, and restaining the wood. If the surface is already finished, color the glue spot to match.

Glue spots, areas where glue smeared onto the surface of the wood, are usually found around joints. When glue dries, it acts like finish in that it seals wood. Consequently, stain can't get through to the wood, and the result is a lighter-colored patch that appears to be unstained. You'll usually see spots as soon as you apply stain, and that's the best time to fix the problem. Stop and wipe off any wet stain. Scrape off the glue with a scraper or razor blade, then sand the area. Sand with the same grit of paper used prior to staining. Restain the area, and if you have all the glue off, it should take color the same way as the rest of the piece.

If you catch glue spots while staining, stop, scrape off the glue, sand, and restain the area.

If you have already applied the finish, the only alternative is to darken the glue spots. Use furniture touchup markers or touchup paints to color the glue spots to match the surrounding finish. Often you can use the stain itself as a touchup paint. Apply it with a fine artist's brush, let it dry thoroughly, and then add another thin coat of finish over the whole piece to seal in your repair.

In the future, check for glue spots before you stain by wetting the entire piece with mineral spirits. This will darken the wood enough to show where the glue is hiding, providing an opportunity to scrape or sand it off before you stain. Once the mineral spirits dry, they have no effect on the wood and won't leave a residue.

Color glue spots after the finish is on with touchup colors or more of the same stain.

Q How can I bring back the sheen to the finish on top of a dressing table that has dull spots on it from spilled perfume?

A Sand out the dull marks with ultrafine sandpaper, then rub the finish to satin or gloss.

Perfume contains alcohol, and alcohol can etch both shellac and lacquer finishes, leaving the finish dull. Fortunately, alcohol evaporates very quickly, usually before it does too much damage. As a result, perfume marks are often superficial and can be removed if the finish is thick enough, and on store-bought furniture, it usually is. Sand the finish with ultrafine 600-grit or finer sandpaper until the spots disappear. Restore the original sheen by rubbing with 0000 steel wool and paste wax for a satin sheen, or with automotive polishing compound for gloss. For a more permanent fix, add a coat of alcohol-proof oil-based polyurethane to the top.

You can often rub out perfume spots on a satin finish with 0000 steel wool and paste wax.

Q What solvent will remove nail polish from a kitchen table?

A Acetone will work, but that could dissolve the finish. Scraping is a safer alternative.

Nail polish is lacquer, and lacquer redissolves itself by melting into one thick, indistinguishable layer. Therefore, nail polish could eat through a lacquer finish by blending into it and making it unrepairable, short of refinishing. Acetone, the solvent in nail polish remover, will also remove lacquer. Test a hidden area to see if acetone dissolves the finish. If it doesn't, use acetone to remove the polish. Otherwise, carefully scrape off the polish with a single-edged razor blade. Try not to remove the clear finish below. Scraping will leave a dull spot; sand it with 600-grit paper and rub the finish back up to satin or gloss to restore the sheen.

Let the nail polish dry, then scrape it off carefully with a single-edge razor blade.

Q I've already applied the topcoat finish, but the color didn't come out right. Is there anything I can do?

A *There is a solution if you want the finish to appear darker. Options include brushed tinted varnish, sprayed toners, and glaze under a topcoat, but all these finishes require some skill to apply.*

There are several options if you want to darken the color of the topcoat finish. In theory, these options will also work to adjust the color to become lighter, but in practice you'll find that light stain over dark has a muddy appearance.

You can change the color of a finished piece by spraying tinted toner on top of the coating.

Restaining or glazing atop the finish also lets you change the color of an already finished piece.

The simple method to fix color is to apply a coat of tinted varnish or lacquer, called toner, on top of the existing finish. Toner is clear coating to which pigment or dye has been added. Dye-based toner is more translucent and won't readily hide the grain of the wood. Pigment-based toner will start to look like paint if you apply too much. Both are available in brushable formulas (such as Minwax Polyshades) or in spray cans from woodworking stores and mail-order outlets that offer Behlen products.

Using toner requires some skill, since you will be applying a coat of colored topcoat to an existing finish. Unless you brush or spray the toner very evenly, you can have spotty or streaked color on your furniture. In most cases, these coatings are not reversible, so you must get it right the first time. Start by cleaning and lightly sanding the surface, then apply the finish as evenly as possible in thin coats. Adding a clear topcoat is optional.

Another option is to apply wood stain or glaze on top of the finish. Both give you more time to manipulate the color to make it uniform and can be wiped off while still wet. You must add a coat of clear finish atop them after they dry completely.

Why is the finish still sticky inside of a cedar chest I finished several months ago with polyurethane?

Cedar can inhibit the cure of some finishes and soften other coatings over time.

Some woods contain chemicals that make them incompatible with certain finishes. Cedar and rosewood, for example, inhibit the curing of oil-based finishes. The oils in cedar can also soften already-cured finishes over time. To fix this problem, remove the existing finish with stripper and apply shellac or Zinsser SealCoat. Those coatings will cure on both cedar and rosewood. However, since the purpose of the cedar in chests is to chase moths and add aroma, it makes more sense to leave it unfinished. Lightly sand the wood's surface now and again to renew the fragrance and appearance.

How do I fill the chips in the thick, clear finish on my sideboard?

Fill chipped areas with cyanoacrylate (super glue adhesive), clear nail polish, or epoxy.

You can fill the voids with several drops of cyanoacrylate (super glue adhesive), clear nail polish, or even epoxy. Cyanoacrylate comes in a container designed to dispense one or two drops at a time. Use a toothpick or small artist's brush to add drops of nail polish or epoxy to the void. When using epoxy, mix it thoroughly, and work quickly before it starts to thicken.

Fill the void with one or two drops of material until it is just barely proud, and let it dry thoroughly. Nail polish will shrink while drying, so you may have to add more. Cyanoacrylate and epoxy will not shrink. Sand the filler flush to the surrounding surface with 400-grit sandpaper, then remove the sanding scratches by resanding with 600-grit paper. To restore the sheen, polish the area with automotive polishing compound.

Use drops of cyanoacrylate (super glue adhesive) or clear nail polish to fill chips in thick, clear finishes.

Can I remove the white rings on my coffee table, where guests placed wet glasses?

Remove white rings by wiping them with a cloth damp with alcohol.

Plants, wet glasses, and hot plates of food can leave white water rings on lacquer finishes. To fix this, mop up any standing water, then let the surface dry completely. Wipe the area gently with a clean cloth dampened with denatured alcohol. Make sure the cloth is only damp, not wet. Always remember that for use on furniture and wood, a damp cloth should feel only as wet as a healthy dog's nose. Wipe the finish gently and quickly, and don't press or rub the finish, as that may cause damage. The rings should come out immediately, but if not, repeat the wiping until they do. If this process leaves the surface looking dull, restore it by rubbing with 0000 steel wool and paste wax for satin finishes, or use automotive polishing compound for gloss finishes.

Remove white rings by wiping them with a cloth dampened with alcohol. The cloth should be damp, not wet.

Dark rings, which are located under the finish and in the wood, not within the finish, are usually impossible to remove, even after stripping.

We had a plant on our sideboard for years. Now there's a dark ring where it sat. Can that be removed?

Dark rings are usually permanent, and lie deep within the wood. Sometimes they can be removed by refinishing the piece.

Dark rings, which typically show up under old or very thin finishes, are not in the finish, but rather in the wood below. They go deep into the wood, and can't be easily sanded out.

Try this. Remove the finish and lightly sand the wood. Flood the surface with a 6 percent solution of oxalic acid crystals (sold as wood bleach) in warm water and let it dry overnight. Remove the white residue with plenty of clean water. If the stain is not gone, apply full-strength laundry bleach, and let it dry. In most cases, the stain will get lighter, but won't entirely disappear.

How can I hide little nicks and scratches on my furniture?

Use scratch cover, touchup markers, and wax sticks to color scratches and fill nicks.

Sometimes just adding color where it is missing, or filling in depressions, is enough to hide the scratches and wear on furniture that is otherwise in good shape. That's where scratch cover, touch-up markers, and wax fill sticks for wood come in handy.

Scratch cover, available in most home stores, is a liquid furniture polish that contains pigment. It hides minor scratches by depositing color in them as you polish the furniture. Choose one that matches the color of your furniture. Use touchup markers or wax fill sticks to repair whatever the scratch cover misses.

Touchup markers look like ordinary felt-tip markers, but they come in common furniture finish colors. Use them just as you would a marker, coloring in areas of your wood furniture where the color has been scratched or rubbed off. Most home improvement and paint stores will have a limited supply of colors, but you'll find a larger assortment in woodworking specialty outlets and catalogs. If you don't find the color you need at the local store, check www.hbehlen.com for sources of both markers and wax fill sticks.

Coloring scratches makes them virtually disappear, but when there are nicks, you'll need to fill them as well. Wax fill sticks look like crayons in furniture finish colors. Choose a color that matches your furniture and rub the stick over the nick until it fills the void completely. Use a credit card to scrape off the excess wax above and around the nick, then burnish the area with a piece of coarse brown-bag paper. In a pinch, you can use kids' crayons, provided you can find the right color.

Use scratch cover or touchup markers to color in damage that goes through the finish.

Fill voids with colored furniture wax sticks, then level the excess with a credit card.

Maintaining and Caring for Finishes

Q How long does a finish take to fully cure and how long should I wait before applying paste wax?

A *Coatings have varying cure times, though some finishes can be waxed before they are cured.*

It is important to understand that *drying time*—the amount of time before a coating is dry to the touch—is not the same as *cure time*. Most coatings dry to the touch in anywhere from a few minutes to a few hours, but almost none of them come to full cure in less than a week. Curiously, some of the fastest-drying finishes, like the water-based coatings, can take the longest to develop the chemical resistance properties that allow them to be waxed without causing problems.

A secondary but equally important issue is that some waxes contain harsher chemicals than others. Briwax, for instance, contains a small amount of toluene, which will etch some water-based finishes that are less than a month old. However, the new Briwax 2000 formula is free of toluene. Some automotive waxes may also be too harsh for fresh finishes. Although there isn't any hard and fast general rule, here is a chart of typical dry times (per coat), cure times (for a typical multicoat finish), and wax times for the most common finish categories. Note that oil and Danish oil have a relatively short cure time in spite of a long drying time, because these two oils are usually applied in very thin coatings.

CURE TIMES FOR COMMON FINISHES

	DRY TIME PER COAT	CURE TIME	WAX AFTER:
Shellac/lacquer	10 minutes	3 weeks	1 day
Water-based	20 minutes	4 weeks	4 weeks
Oil/Danish oil/ polyurethane	Overnight	1 week	2 days
Varnish	4–6 hours	6 weeks	2 days
Conversion varnish	10 minutes	8 days	1 day

Can I use auto polish or paste wax from the auto supply store on furniture?

Yes, you can, provided the finish is fully cured.

Some auto polishes and paste waxes contain solvents that might be a bit hard on fresh water-based finishes, but besides that, you should have no problem.

If you give the finish ample cure time, you can use automotive products on furniture. I often buy rubbing and polishing compounds from the auto parts store. Be warned that some automotive liquid polishes and waxes contain silicone, which can make refinishing more problematic. However, silicone will not harm or prematurely age a cured finish—its presence only becomes a concern when it is time to refinish.

Here are a few of my favorite automotive rubbing and polishing compounds, all purchased at the auto store.

Are there differences between paste waxes? Are certain waxes better on some finishes than others?

There are minor differences between paste waxes, but you can apply any wax over any finish.

Paste waxes help shed water, add a silky feel, and may reduce scratches on a finish by adding some slip to the surface. Some are softer and easier to apply, some dry faster, some buff up more easily, and some smell better. Choosing a paste wax is largely a matter of personal preference. While some paste waxes are a bit harder or softer than others, all of them are softer than the finishes they purport to protect. The major differences between waxes are in their working properties, not durability.

Perhaps what's more important is that they are universal and that any paste wax can go over any finish. Choose the wax with the consistency, working properties, price, and smell that appeals to you.

Q **What is toluene and will it damage finishes?**

Toluene is a common finishing solvent that could etch some finishes.

For many years, toluene was sold as "liquid sandpaper" because of its ability to etch or bite into the surface of certain finishes. Though it will have little effect on oil-based coatings like varnish and polyurethane, it could eat into some lacquers and water-based materials, especially if the finish is fresh. In fact, toluene is one of the three solvents that make up refinisher, a mixture designed to re-knit, or gently remove, lacquer and shellac.

While toluene is not strong enough to act as a paint remover or dissolve a finish by itself, it can reduce the sheen and leave a finish looking dull. Consequently, it is not a good solvent for cleaning wood furniture.

Q **It is okay to polish fine furniture with Murphy's Oil Soap?**

I think you mean clean, since Murphy's Oil Soap is a cleaner, not a polish, but it is certainly an acceptable cleaner.

Most film-forming finishes, like lacquer, shellac, varnish, and polyurethane, are designed to protect wood, and other than keeping them clean, they require no further maintenance. The best thing you can use to clean wood furniture is mild soap and water, which will take off dirt without harming the finish. Murphy's Oil Soap is just such a product, an effective but mild soap. It is a fine choice for your routine cleaning chores.

Murphy's Oil Soap is an effective but gentle soap appropriate for cleaning any finished furniture.

Q Will glass cleaner hurt an antique wood finish?

A Glass cleaner can hurt some finishes, and therefore it is not appropriate for cleaning antiques.

I do not recommend using glass cleaner, or any other ammonia-based cleaner, for cleaning fine wood furniture or antiques. Instead, use mild soap and water or commercial furniture cleaner.

Some glass cleaners contain ammonia or other chemicals which give them a high pH, also known as being alkaline. Shellac, a common finish on antiques as well as on handmade furniture, is resistant to acids, but breaks down in the presence of an alkaline substance such as ammonia. If the glass cleaner contains enough ammonia, it can eat a shellac finish right off the wood. Some water-based lacquers are also sensitive to alkalines, especially when the finish is fairly fresh. Oil-based varnishes and polyurethane finishes are impervious to alkalines, so you can get away with using a glass cleaner on those coatings.

Any cleaners that contain ammonia, such as certain glass cleaners, can soften, damage, or remove shellac finishes.

Q What is lemon oil? I've seen lemon oil furniture polish advertised as ideal for rejuvenating old wood furniture.

A Lemon oil is scented mineral oil. It is harmless, and has both advantages and disadvantages.

Lemon scent, either synthetic or natural, is sometimes added to mineral oil to make it more pleasant-smelling. Mineral oil is a nondrying oil, so if you spread it on your furniture, it will leave a thin oil film that makes the surface shiny, which appeals to many people. Unfortunately, the oil doesn't dry, so it tends to collect dust, making it necessary to frequently repolish.

My furniture looks dull and hazy from numerous coats of paste wax. Is there some way of removing the wax buildup?

VM&P naphtha, paired with fine 0000 steel wool, will do the job.

Remove old wax from wood with special wax removers, or simply use VM&P naphtha.

Over time, wax can build up enough to get thick and dull, catch dirt, and feel tacky. Since wax resists water, washing with soap and water may not remove it. VM&P naphtha, the solvent for paste wax, will remove wax, dirt, lemon oil, mineral oil, and other furniture polish residues, and it won't harm any wood finish.

Use ultrafine 0000 steel wool and plenty of naphtha to clean a satin finish. The steel wool will help dislodge the wax more quickly and will restore the satin sheen. However, even fine steel wool will dull a gloss finish. On gloss finishes, use naphtha on a coarse cloth instead of steel wool. The naphtha will create a slurry of solvent, dirt, and wax. Wipe it up with clean paper towels and repeat the process until the towels look clean, or until you are satisfied with the appearance of the finish.

The finish on my coffee table is starting to wear. Is there something I can do to extend its life?

Recoat the piece of furniture with a layer or two of the original finish.

Recoating wood will extend an old finish's life. Either SealCoat or oil-based polyurethane (liquid or gel) is compatible and will adhere to any finish.

Finishes wear as furniture gets used. Though you can't prevent that, you can certainly rejuvenate a finish now and again with an additional coat or two of whatever coating was originally applied to the piece of furniture. To do that, first remove any wax, dirt, and polish (see above), and let the surface dry. When it is dry, sand the surface very lightly with 400-grit sandpaper. Wipe off the sanding dust with a damp cloth, and apply another coat or two of finish. If you are not sure what the original finish was, Zinsser SealCoat, or any oil-based polyurethane, can go safely over any finish.

I put several coats of Danish oil on a piece I built, and I'd like it to keep looking good. How do I maintain it?

Clean the surface with mild soap and water, add paste wax once or twice a year, and add extra Danish oil when needed.

As with all finishes, keep the Danish oil finish clean by washing the piece of furniture with mild soap and water, and if you'd like, adding a coat of paste wax once or twice a year.

The problem with Danish oil, as well as with tung oil and boiled linseed oil is that these coatings are usually applied thin. As a result, the Danish oil is more likely to wear prematurely as abrasion erodes the finish through to the wood.

When the finish starts to look dry or worn, remove any wax or polish (see p. 131) and add another coat or two of Danish oil. Apply it liberally with a fine nylon abrasive pad, then wipe it off evenly with shop towels. This adds a thin new coat, but avoids brush marks. Add two or three coats every few years, and your furniture will keep its good looks indefinitely. **Warning: Oily towels are spontaneously combustible. Lay them out one layer thick and let them dry completely before disposing of them.**

Renew a Danish oil finish by applying extra coats whenever it starts to show signs of wear.

Lay oily rags out one layer thick. It's important to let them dry completely before adding them to the household trash.

The Danish oil finish on my kitchen table looks great, but it doesn't wear well. How can I make it more durable?

Clean the table and upgrade the finish with a couple of coats of oil-based polyurethane.

Fortunately, Danish oil is fully compatible with oil-based polyurethane. Clean off any wax, grease, or dirt with naphtha and steel wool, then brush on two or three thin coats of oil-based polyurethane. It will look great and still be tough enough to handle anything from food stains and hot coffee pots to solvents and abrasions.

Q Can I restore dry wood without losing the patina?

A Dry wood restores itself when placed in a room with proper relative humidity, but you can restore a finish without harming the patina.

Long after it has been cut and fashioned into furniture, wood continues to move. As the conditions around it change, it absorbs moisture from the air, or releases it, again and again, swelling or shrinking with changes in humidity. This process goes on indefinitely in spite of the finish on the wood. All you need do to restore dry wood is to humidify the room where the furniture sits.

If your wood furniture looks dry, you may be witnessing the deterioration of the finish. Over time, finishes get progressively thinner, weaker, and more brittle until they check and crack. Some of the checking, which consists of fine crack lines running parallel to the grain, is due to the movement of the wood beneath the finish.

The word patina refers to the greenish film formed naturally on copper or bronze that is exposed to air. Wood aficionados use the word to describe the elusive beauty that wood develops

This newly sanded piece of walnut is much darker than the sun-faded patina of this old walnut box.

with age. When exposed to light, wood gets more translucent, and goes through changes in color, depth, and chatoyance (shimmer). A finish can also change color when it is exposed to light, so at least some of what we call patina is in the finish.

You can rejuvenate a finish by adding more coats of the same material. That won't destroy the patina. When you must refinish, you can save some of the patina by stripping with chemicals and avoiding sanding the wood. You'll lose the aged, checked finish, but you'll save the patina intrinsic to the wood.

Q How can I tell what kind of finish is on an old piece of furniture?

A You can't tell exactly what finish is on an old piece of furniture, but you can narrow it down to the general category of finish.

Place a drop of solvent on a cotton gun patch and cover it with a watch glass as a test to identify the type of finish.

Although it seems like a simple question, the answer is rather complicated. Because finishes share many characteristics, it is not always possible to pinpoint the exact type of finish on a piece of furniture without sophisticated chemical testing equipment. However, a few simple solvent tests combined with visual clues and a knowledge of history can get you into the ballpark.

Finishes fall into two broad categories: evaporative and reactive. Evaporative finishes will redissolve in their own solvent. In other words, alcohol will dissolve shellac and lacquer thinner will soften lacquer. Reactive finishes will not redissolve once cured. Soak a gun patch or a tiny square of cotton fabric in denatured alcohol and place it on the finish under a watch glass, preferably in an inconspicuous area. Check it in about a minute. If the finish becomes softened and the cloth sticks to it, then it is shellac. The same test, using lacquer thinner, will identify the finish as either solvent or water-based lacquer. If it responds to neither, it is a reactive finish.

Although specific finish test kits exist, they are hard to find outside museum conservation labs. Fortunately, history and visual clues can help. Prior to 1960, oil-based varnishes were the only reactive finishes commonly used on furniture. Modern reactives include two-part urethanes, epoxy, and polyester, all of which pass the alcohol/lacquer thinner test. Oil varnishes are usually more amber, though dye added to clear finish makes identification difficult.

Q Is there a way to repair the alligatoring in an old finish?

Yes, but it's risky because it requires amalgamator, a material that takes a good bit of practice to master.

Some finishes alligator as they get old. That means the finish shrinks and develops surface cracks in a pattern of squares that looks almost identical to alligator skin. The cracks may only appear partway through the finish, or they may go deep, all the way down to the wood. A mixture of solvents, called amalgamator, has the ability to redissolve and soften the finish, allowing a technician to reblend the softened finish and restore it to its formerly smooth surface.

Amalgamator is only sold to professional restorers, and for good reason. You can find a source for amalgamator at www.hbehlen.com. Unless you have a lot of experience with French polish techniques, amalgamator is as likely to damage, remove, or curdle the finish as it is to reknit it. One finishing instructor told me he'd sooner let his 10-year-old drive his car as put amalgamator in the hands of a novice. That is a sentiment worth heeding. However, if you are tempted to try amalgamator, practice first on a piece that you are willing to refinish. That way, if things go awry, you can always strip off the finish and apply a new one.

To reknit the finish, apply amalgamator to a pad and gently rub it on the surface. The solvents soften the finish while the pressure and movement of the pad redistributes the softened coating. If it's done correctly, the cracked surface becomes smooth. But it takes skill, patience, and time to gradually work the surface back to its former glory without replacing or adding any finish.

Amalgamator can reknit an old, alligatored finish, but it involves a technique best left to people experienced in finish repair.

Index

Wood Finishing Fixes